TROIA

NURTEN SEVİNÇ
(Curator of Çanakkale Archaeological Museum)

A T U R İ Z M Y A Y I N L A R I

Editor
Fatih Cimok

Cover design
Suat Ataç

Graphics
Feryal Özbay

Photographs
Cüneyt Baykurt & Tahsin Aydoğmuş

Filmset
Çali Grafik

Printed at
Asır Matbaası

First printing July 1992
Second revised printing March 1996

Publishers
A Turizm Yayınları Ltd. Şti.
Şifa Hamamı Sokak 18/2, Sultanahmet 34400, İstanbul
Tel: 516 24 97, 517 44 72, 517 44 74; Fax: 516 41 65

CONTENTS

INTRODUCTION   5

SIGHTSEEING IN TROIA
Trojan horse   9
East tower, east fortification wall and east gate (Troia VI)   11
Megaron houses (Troia VI)   16
Temple of Athena (Troia VIII & Troia IX)   24
Northeast tower (water tower) and cistern (Troia VI)   25
Great theatre (Troia IX)   25
Fortification walls, tower and megaron houses (Troia I)   26
Monumental gate, megaron palace,
ramp and fortification walls (Troia II)   29
West gate VIU (Troia VI)   36
Troia III   37
Troia IV   37
Troia V   38
VIM building (Troia VI)   39
Troia VIII   40
Sacred precinct   41
Troia IX   42
Nymphaeum (monumental fountain) (Troia IX)   44
Little theatre (Troia IX)   45
South gate (Troia VI)   46
Pillar house (Troia VI)   47
Bouleterion (council house) (Troia IX)   49

DISCOVERY OF TROIA, HEINRICH SCHLIEMANN and TREASURE   50

TROJAN WAR   54

VISITORS TO TROIA   62

ÇANAKKALE ARCHAEOLOGICAL MUSEUM   63

INTRODUCTION

The main objective of this small volume is to give practical information about the ruins of Troia, which look very confusing to visitors at first sight, and to help them understand the history of Troia easily.

Instead of narrating the chronological history of all nine cities which were founded here, the ruins are introduced in the order of the sightseeing itinerary. When the visitor begins the sighseeing tour here, the first thing which catches his eye is a giant wooden horse, then the first ruins he comes across are those of Troia VI, and thus these are introduced first and the rest of the ruins are dealt with in the same practical manner.

The story of the discovery of Troia is one of the most exciting adventures in the history of archaeology. The life of the man who discovered Troia, the treasure he found, the rumours which followed its loss, its rediscovery in the vaults of Puskin Museum in Moscow have given Troia a special place among the sites of antiquity in Anatolia. However, unless one is well acquainted with the history of the site or has a rich imagination, the impression given by the present condition of the ruins may be one of disappointment. Little is left from the ancient glories of King Priam, and the high towers and walls, palaces and temples of

Homer have perished. When one realizes that nine separate cities of altogether forty settlement layers were founded on the same spot, as well as the fact that the very early excavations were not carried out in a scientific way, the difficulty of understanding and interpreting the surviving ruins of Troia will become obvious.

This guide book makes no attempt to deal with the historical and archaeological arguments whether the Trojan war ever actually happened, or if it did, at which particular settlement. The Trojan war is simplified like the history of the site and presented in a practical manner.

Each of the five chapters in this book deals with a different aspect of Troia and may be read and enjoyed separately. It is obvious that the original Greek name of the city 'Troia' – which was used by Homer – has been preferred in the contemporary vogue of using the original names for ancient sites. The quotations about the Trojan war are taken from the latest translation of the *Iliad* (Penguin Classics, 1991) by Robert Eagles. The same volume is referred to for the spelling of Greek names. For the illustrations of the heroes of the Trojan war, their depictions on various antique pots have been used. The mythological information is based on the *Greek Myths* by Robert Graves.

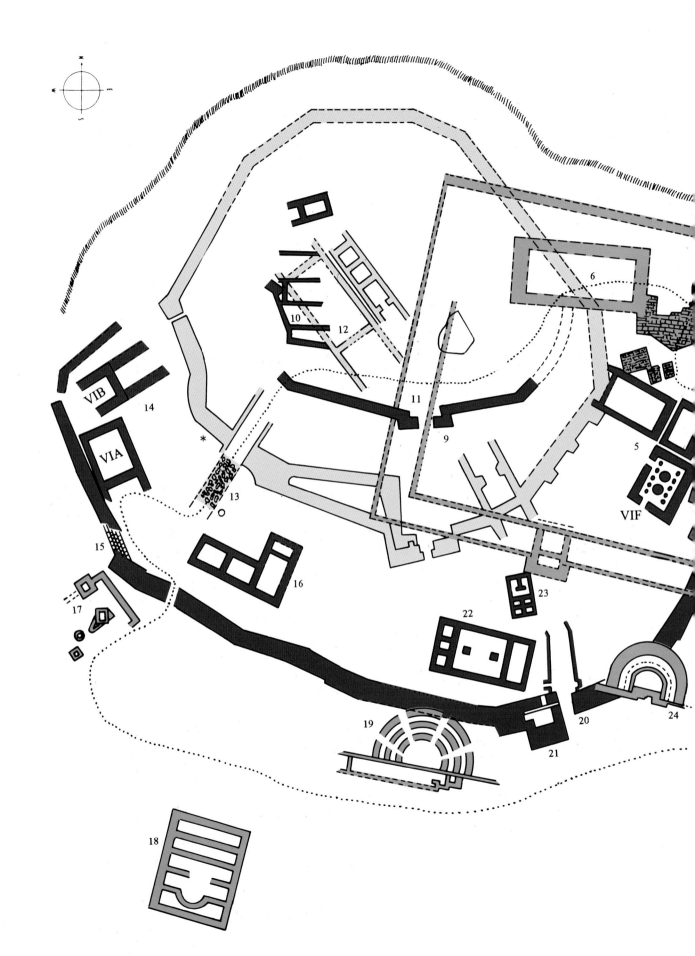

VIB

VIA

14

*

13

10

12

11

9

6

5

VIF

15

17

16

23

22

20

24

21

19

18

PLAN OF TROIA. THE DOTS INDICATE
THE PRESENT SIGHTSEEING ROUTE.

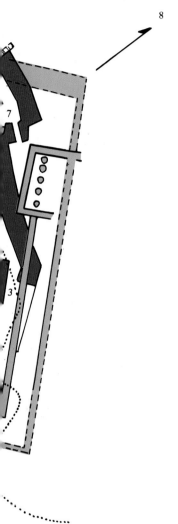

SIGHTSEEING ROUTE
and
RUINS OF TROIA

1 - East tower (Troia VI)
2 - East wall (Troia VI)
3 - East gate (Dardanian Gates?) (Troia VI)
4 - Storage rooms (Troia VIIa)
5 - Megaron houses (Troia VI)
6 - Temple of Athena (Troia VIII & Troia IX)
7 - Northeast tower and cistern (Troia VI)
8 - Great theatre (Troia IX)
9 - City gate, east tower and wall (Troia I)
10 - Megaron houses (Troia I)
11 - City gate (Troia II)
12 - Megaron palace (Troia II)
13 - Ramp and wall (Troia II)
   * Spot where Schliemann discovered 'treasure'
14 - Megaron houses (Troia VI)
15 - West gate VIU (Troia VI)
16 - VIM building (Troia VI)
17 - Sacred precinct
18 - Monumental fountain (Troia IX)
19 - Little theatre (Troia IX)
20 - South gate (Scaean Gates?) (Troia VI)
21 - Great tower (Troia VI)
22 - Pillar house (Troia VI)
23 - House 630 (Troia VI)
24 - Council house (Troia IX)

TROIA I (3000–2500 BC)
TROIA II (2500–2200 BC)
TROIA VI (1800–1275 BC)
TROIA VIIa (1275–1240 BC)
TROIA VIII (700–350 BC) & TROIA IX (350 BC – 400 AD)

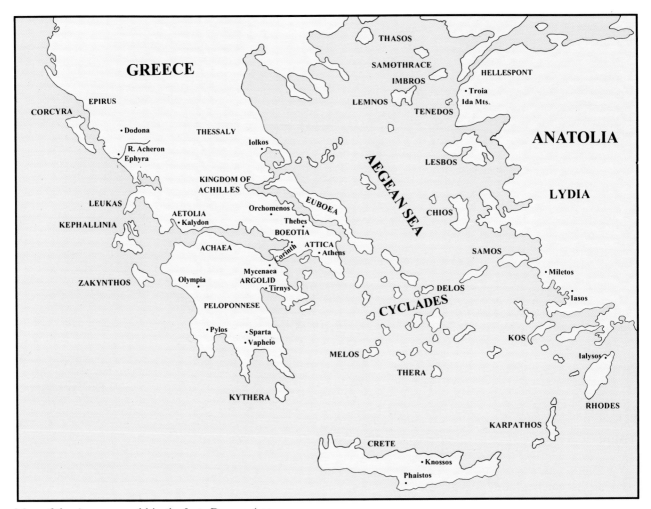

Map of the Aegean world in the Late Bronze Age

Detail from the 'warrior vase' from Mycenae. Late thirteenth century BC. National Museum, Athens. It shows a Mycenaean warrior armed with a small shield and a spear. He is dressed in a chiton and carries a short breast plate and helmet. The Achaeans who destroyed Troia VIIa (1275–1240 BC) are thought to have been armed like this warrior.

Marble pedestal of the statue of the Roman tribune Lucius Vinuleius Pataecius situated near the model wooden horse. Troia IX (350 BC–400 AD). The inscription in Greek relates that the monument is dedicated to the soldier, who served as a cavalry commander within the frontiers of the Empire of Caesar Augustus Vespasianus (67–79 AD) in Africa, Asia and Thracia, by the senate and the people. Ancient sources give no information about the person to whom the dedication is made.

SIGHTSEEING IN TROIA
Trojan horse

When one approaches the ruins of Troia today, the first thing that catches the eye is a giant wooden horse. This has been constructed from the pine trees of the Ida mountains as was the original wooden horse of the Trojan war. Today, the horse helps to enliven the imagination of children '– and probably of adults as well – about the legend. It was constructed in 1974 and has become a symbol of ancient Troia ever since. When the horse was built, in order to ensure its close proximity to the original, reference was made to the depictions on antique pottery and descriptions of ancient writers. Its size relates to the original fortifications of the city of the Trojan war.

If the story of the Trojan horse is recalled, the Achaeans abandon hope of taking the city by force, and building a wooden horse they dedicate it to the goddess Athena who gave them this idea. Afterwards, they break camp, board their ships and hide themselves in the bays of the island Tenedos (present day Bozcaada belonging to Turkey). At daybreak, the Trojans, when they see no sign of the enemy, think that the Achaeans are disprited by the fruitless ten year siege and have decided to return home. They begin to celebrate their victory, even though their seer of Apollo, Laocoon

Detail from the reliefs depicting the capture of Lachish by King Sennacherib of Assyria. *c* 695 BC. British Museum, London. It shows an Assyrian siege engine with a protective leather covering, fastened with toggles. While a fireman inside ladles water to prevent it being set alight by incendiary darts sodiers in the siege engine try to demolish the gate tower with a giant spear, worked from inside.

Detail from the vertical earthquake cracks on the wall of the east tower, facing towards the gate. Troia VI (1800–1275 BC)

warns them that nothing good will come from a gift dedicated to Athena, who throughout the war supported the Achaeans. His warnings are ignored and the horse is pulled into the city on tree trunks. The gate by which the horse is taken inside is too small and it has to be removed – to be reconstructed immediately once the horse is inside. At midnight, when the moon is high in the sky and the Trojans, including the sentries, are asleep, exhausted from the celebrations, the Achaeans open the trap door and climb out of the horse. They kill the sleeping guards, open the gates and signal their friends with torches. This is the beginning of the end of Troia.

Experts on this subject interpret the story of the Trojan horse in a number of different ways. Some believe that the story was probably inspired by the siege engines used by the Assyrians and depicted in their reliefs going back to the seventh century BC. In these reliefs, Assyrian soldiers hidden in three-wheeled siege engines are shown trying to demolish fortifications of the enemy by using battering rams. Although such vehicles are not encountered in records of Aegean warfare, it has been suggested that the Achaeans might have used a similar tower-like siege engine covered with wet horse hides to protect it against catching fire. Nevertheless, the archaeological examination of the fortifications of Troia VI – large blocks of fallen stone and vertical cracks in the walls – indicates that shortly before the city was burned, it had suffered a major earthquake, and thus the Achaeans probably did not find it difficult to breach the already weakened walls and sack the city. After the city falls, they build a horse dedicated to the god Poseidon, the *Earthshaker*, who supported them during the war and who was believed to have caused the earthquake, Poseidon represented and was worshipped in the Hellenic world in the shape of a horse – 'hippos'.

The marble columns, inscribed pedestals and other construction materials seen around the wooden horse today come from the earliest excavations at Troia or have been gathered from the fields. The large baked clay jars which were used for storing food such as wheat, wine or olive oil, come from the ruins of the settlement which was built immediately after the city of Troia VI and is labelled by the archaeologists as Troia VIIa (1275–1240 BC). The baked clay pipe pieces lying on the ground were part of the irrigation system which brought water to Troia from the Ida mountains during the Hellenistic and Roman periods.

East tower, fortificaion wall, gate and – in the background – megaron houses. Troia VI (1800–1275 BC)

East tower, east fortification wall and east gate

Troia VI (1800–1275 BC)

When one reaches the beginning of the actual sightseeing area, the flat top of the small hill* on the right is the best spot to get a bird's eye view of the eastern part of the ciadel of Troia VI (1800–1275 BC).

Excavations have revealed that in about 1800 BC – at the time when the Hittites were penetrating into Anatolia – Troia was also settled, by people of a different culture to those of the previous settlements. The people of this new stock surrounded the city with large impregnable fortifications. Although nothing is known about their origins and language, their characteristic architecture such as monumental gates protected with towers, large megaron houses like palaces, and strong walls, as well as similarities in the baked clay pottery, give the impression that these new settlers of Troia must have been related to the emigrants who penetrated mainland Greece from the north during the same period. A horse skeleton and other horse

bones which were found in excavations indicate the popularity of the animal during this period and recall the expressions used by Homer for the Trojans such as, *horse-taming Trojans* or *Ilios, famed for its horses*. It can be concluded in the light of the research carried out in this part of Anatolia, that during this period of history some new stock of people, who used horses and horse-drawn chariots in war, utilized bronze weapons, and also built strong fortifications, arrived in Troia, and took over the Troas region.

In the foreground, the most impressive ruins of Troia VI – the east tower, the east wall and the east gate – catch the eye. Behind these, on a terrace, the ruins of megaron houses rise.

The tower, walls and the gate are the best examples of the defense system of Troia VI and the finest for the time they were built in the whole ancient world. The walls are vertical inside, sloping in towards the top outside* and are built of rectangular porous limestone blocks without any mortar between them. Their outward face is extremely smooth to make climbing impossible. Their size is not large. The length is longer than the height. They are shaped like bricks and give

---

* When one walks down by the narrow path leading to the valley from the front of this artificial hill, one can reach the bottom of the northeast tower and the ruins of the great theatre.

* This feature is common to the walls of the previous settlements and not encountered elsewhere in western Anatolia.

East tower. Troia VI (1800–1275 BC)

East tower. Wall with the earthquake cracks

Offsets from the east fortification wall

East gate (Dardanian Gates?) with the overlapping walls. Troia VI (1800–1275 BC)

the impression that smaller sized blocks were preferred. The stonework is irregular, making one think that they were cut and shaped individually before the wall was built. This section of the walls is divided vertically into five parts by perpendicular shallow offsets of 10 to 15 cm at about every 10 m. The offsets show the slight changes of direction in the wall and indicate that it did not have any corners, i.e. any towers, which were always a weak point in any defensive system and were often undermined in any enemy attack. This is the reason why in the architecture of Troia VI towers are used only for guarding gates. Including the upper section, which was made of sun-dried mudbricks reinforced with wooden beams, these walls are thought to have reached a height of about 12.5 m. Even today their lower stone sections have survived up to approximately 4.5 m. It is thought that at the top there was originally a parapet and running along behind this a narrow platform along which guards patrolled. The water tunnel which is made from sandstone blocks and is located at ground level opposite the fortifications is from the Roman period.

The entrance of the east gate has a corridor 5 m in length and 2 m wide which was originally protected by the overlapping walls on both of its sides. This corridor enabled the inhabitants to defend this entrance by crossfiring at the enemy using arrows, spears and boulders from both sides. The actual entrance between the walls is not located opposite the corridor but on the left side, and this was a further obstacle for the enemy trying to force the city from this side. The function of the east tower, located some distance away from this gate was to prevent the enemy from gathering at the back of the narrow entrance*.

A careful eye will notice that the wall on the right side of the corridor is different from the original wall on the left. This is a part or the wall of the sacred enclosure (temenos) which surrounded the temple of Athena. It is Roman and rests on a part of the defensive wall of the gate. When its weak workmanship and soft limestone material are compared with that the parallel

* The cracks which are thought to have resulted from the previously mentioned earthquake have survived on the tower wall facing towards the entrance.

East fortification wall. Troia VI (1800–1275 BC)

Wall belonging to the sacred enclosure of the temple of
Athena (built on the outer wall of the east gate of Troia VI).
Troia IX (350 BC – 400 AD)

wall built approximately 1500 years before, the strength
of the fortifications of Troia VI can be appreciated
more easily. The strong character of these walls gives
the impression that they must have been built when
Troia VI was at the zenith of its power – between 1400
and 1325 BC –, and experts think that the entrance
located here might have been the *Dardanian Gates* of
the *Iliad*. At one stage of the war Hera encourages
the Achaeans saying

*'Shame! Disgrace! You Argives, you degraded—
splendid in battle dress, pure sham!
As long as brilliant Achilles stalked the front
no Trojan would ever venture beyond the
Dardanian Gates,
They were so afraid of the man's tremendous spear.
Now they're fighting far away from the city,
right by your hollow ships!'*

The impression one gets from the *Iliad* is that
during the Trojan war, the city was not completely
isolated and contact with the inland region of Troas
was established by this gate.

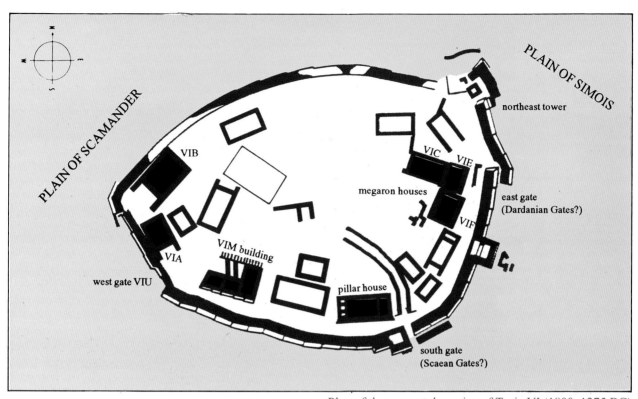

PLAIN OF SCAMANDER

PLAIN OF SIMOIS

VIB

VIC   VIE

northeast tower

megaron houses

east gate
(Dardanian Gates?)

VIF

VIA

VIM building

west gate VIU

pillar house

south gate
(Scaean Gates?)

Plan of the present day ruins of Troia VI (1800–1275 BC)

Citadel of Troia VI (1800-1275 BC) during the Late Bronze Age (illustration Suat Ataç)

Storage rooms of Troia VIIa (1275–1240 BC) (view from east)

Stone base of a wooden column from VIC house. The worn out surface shows that it must have supported a wooden column of diameter of 38 cm. Troia VI (1800–1275 BC)

Megaron houses

Troia VI (1800–1275 BC)

As one enters the city turning to the left and climbing a few stairs, a section of the empty area which once encircled the city all along the walls in the shape of a boulevard can be examined. Along the inner side this area is bordered by the walls of the megaron houses* which shows the same stonework as the fortifications. The weaker vertical walls which divide this narrow corridor into small rooms were built after Troia VI had suffered the earthquake mentioned before and belong to the successive city of Troia VIIa (1275–1240 BC). If the weak stone work of these low walls is compared with those they join, it becomes obvious that people who were familliar with the art of making such strong walls would not have constructed these weak walls unless they were short of time. The large number of these rooms indicates that during this period the population of the city suddenly increased. The big baked clay jars which came from these rooms show that they were used for long term storage as well. Originally, these jars would have been buried in the floor, their mouths at floor level being covered with stone lids. The fact that such storage jars were not found in the houses of Troia VI, but in the successive city VIIa, shows that during this period the population

* A long, narrow, isolated house consisting of one front room as entrance and a hall with a hearth the in centre. For Homer it is a hall with a hearth and where men met.

of the city did not feel safe, and felt it necessary to store food.

At the top of stairs to the south are the remains of the megaron houses of Troia VI. One of the common features of these houses is that their outer walls, facing the city walls, show better workmanship than their other walls. For instance, the outer wall of the first megaron which is known as VIE, of which almost nothing is left except for its outer wall, shows the characteristic stonework of Troia VI. The large VIC house situated immediately at the back of this house (to the west) has been almost completely destroyed by Schliemann's trench. From the fact that this house has a stone base *in situ* in the north-west corner of the room, archaeologists have come to the conclusion that there were two more stone bases and its roof was carried by three columns situated along the longer axis of the room.

The VIF house situated after VIE (to the south) has different features from the other houses. The thickness of its walls is not uniform, the one facing the fortifications being thicker than the others and made of large stone blocks. It has vertical projections on its outer face. The two centrally located large stone column bases and the smaller bases which are laid in rows of five along the longer walls, are thought too many to carry the roof of a room only 8 m in width.

Megaron house VIF. Troia VI (1800–1275 BC) (view from east). The wholes belong to the wooden beams which have not survived

Detail from the stonework of the outer wall of the megaron house VIE of Troia VI (1800–1275 BC)

Consequently, archaeologists think that originally the house had a roof supported by two wooden columns resting on the bases in the centre, and afterwards when a second floor was built the additional ten columns became necessary for extra support. The thin openings to be seen on the walls today would have been the spots where the horizontal and vertical wooden beams which supported the walls were fitted in. During this change, the doorway on the south side was blocked up and a new entrance was built in the west wall. The large stone block seen today next to the earlier blocked up entrance is thought to have served as a base for a wooden staircase which led to the upper floor. The south-west corner of the room has a hearth. The lower part of a jar which was partly buried in the stone floor next to the hearth is thought to have served as a kind of grate. The VIG house situated in the south of VIF has been almost completely destroyed by Schliemann's trench.

The surviving ruins of Troia VI give impression that the city was divided radially into six sections by wide streets starting from five gates on which megaron

Baked clay jar. Mycenaean. Troia VI (1800–1275 BC).
Çanakkale Archaeological Museum

South-west corner of megaron house VIF. Hearth and
stone base. Troia VI (1800–1275 BC)

houses were built. These houses were trapezoidal in shape, with their shorter sides facing the acropolis and their longer sides on the fortification side. In this manner, they follow the line of the acropolis which opens out into a rough fan-shape from north to south, giving the impression that the city of Troia of this period was carefully planned. At the highest point in the city, thought to have been about 40 to 50 m above the valley, the palace of the king, which was probably a large two-storeyed building, must have stood. It was probably another large megaron, whose roof was supported by wooden columns standing on marble or stone bases. It would have had a wooden staircase leading to a bedroom on the upper floor. In the centre of the large room, there would have been a large circular platform with a big hearth serving for both lighting and heating. The smoke would have escaped through a hole in the ceiling. This hearth would have been the heart of the Trojan noble society. The king would have gathered the most important in the land around this hearth, and served them with the meat that he cooked on the fire. The hearth would always have been open to doctors, soothsayers, bards and artisans. Around the hearth, there would have been wooden benches and chairs with backs. These would have been covered with handmade woollen material or animal skins. During meal times, tables would have been brought in front of these seats. Bread in baskets, wine in baked clay jugs, and the meat roasted on the fire would have been served on these small tables. To run the city politically and economically, to correspond with similar kings, to support the merchant ships, and to decide the amount of surplus wool and wheat to be sent to other countries would have been the major preoccupations of the king. He would have had scribes around him and these would have utilized cuneiform or Linear B writing*. The king would have been responsible for the religious ceremonies to be performed before he went to war, or began a journey and on his return from such errands. He would have supervised such rituals for his family and clan as high priest, sacrificing and dedicating gifts to the gods. As well as being a good horseman, he would have been a good huntsman and a good sailor. When younger, he would have tended his flocks personally, like his sons.

* A particular form of writing regarded as the earliest form of the Greek language, also known as Mycenaean Greek. Although its roots are in ideograms, it has an abstract linear form.

When there was no war, hunting would have been his favourite pastime. The region was abundant in wild boar and animals such as leopard. Although he would have had servants and grooms, the king would probably have enjoyed looking after the needs of his own horse. He would have cared for his own weapons and armour. In wartime, he would have ridden a chariot and fought with sword and shield, bow and arrow, and two spears. Such a way of life was common to all contemporary kings who ruled similar kingdoms on mainland Greece and this distinguished them from divine rulers in Mesopotamia and Egypt who were regarded as gods, confined within the walls of their palaces, having no contact with the practical day-to-day life of their subjects. Homer, in his *Iliad*, which is thought to have been composed approximately 400 years after Troia was destroyed, refers to the house of King Priam with the following lines:

And soon he came to Priam's palace, that magnificent structure built wide with porches and colonnades of polished stone. And deep within its walls were fifty sleeping chambers masoned in smooth, lustrous ashlar, linked in a line where the sons of Priam slept beside their wedded wives, and facing these, opening out across the inner courtyard-lay the twelve sleeping chambers of Priam's daughters, masoned and roofed in lustrous ashlar, linked in a line here the sons-in- law of Priam slept beside their wives.

The houses in which the king's relatives lived would have been smaller than that of the king, built side by side and separately, with rectangular plans similar to that of his house. There would have been rooms for storing food, for maintaining weapons, and pens for animals. The grinding of wheat, the sifting of flour and making of bread, the spinning of wool and weaving of materials, these would have been the most important occupations of the women.

The abundance of sheep and goat bones found in excavations, and the number of spindle whorls, indicate that during this period the city had a thriving weaving industry, and this is confirmed by the high number of bone awls, needles and pins found. The remainder of the city population must have been made up of artisans who smelted metals, potters skillful at the wheel, and soldiers. The population occupied with agriculture, animal husbandry and fishing must have been larger than population of the city. Their villages must have occupied the flat piece of land on the sea side. Since the

Tumulus of Hisarlık (view from the plain of Simois)

Wild poppies in the plain of Simois

Plain of Simois (view from the north-east tower)

Mosaic pavement from Defne (Daphne) near Antakya (Antioch-on-the-Orontes). Detail. End of second-beginning of third centuries AD. Hatay Archaeological Museum, Antakya. Zeus' eagle or Zeus, disguised as an eagle is about to abduct Ganymede, son of Tros, the legendary founder of Troia from the plain of Simois.

Scamander River changed its bed and the area was silted no trace is left from these settlements. These people probably took shelter inside the city walls during times of war. The present walls of Troia VI are thought to be large enough to have accommodated a permanent population of approximate 1,000 people within, while another 5,000 people would have been living outside the city.

The Trojan fisherman caught herring, tuna and other fish during their annual migration through the Dardanelles, which is referred to by Homer as *Hellespont that swarms with fish*. It has been claimed that the real cause of the Trojan war might have been the fishing rights at the mouth of Dardanelles and in the Aegean. The Trojan war ships controlled the trade routes connecting the Black Sea to the Aegean and the Mediterranean, and Trojan rulers exacted tax from merchant ships passing through the strait. Although

the harbour had been silted up since foundation of the first city here, at the time of Troia VI – the city was then about 1 km inland – it was still deep enough for merchant ships to drop anchor while they waited for the right prevailing winds. During this period, a spontaneous commercial and cultural exchange must have taken place between the seafaring merchants and the Trojan ruling class.

The objects which have come to light in excavations show that during this period Troia had very intense cultural and trade contacts with Crete and Cyprus, the Aegean Islands and mainland Greece.

After the megaron houses, one reaches the highest

Opposite Cotton harvest in the silted plain of Simois (view from the north-east tower). Beyond the Dardanelles the monuments erected for the soldiers who fell during the World War I are visible.

point of the present tumulus of Hisarlık. This is the best point from which the general topography of the citadel can be examined. Since the entrance to the ruins is on the south-east, until one arrives at this viewpoint it is difficult to appreciate that Troia is a tumulus of forty settlement layers, resting one on top of the other. It is known that the height of the tumulus increased by 5 or 6 m just during the eight layers of Troia VI alone. If the tumulus is seen from the valley its height can be better appreciated. On the left-hand side, the tumulus is bordered by the stream Scamander (Kara Menderes) to the south-west, and on the opposite side by the Simois (Dümrek) to the north-east. Looking at the present conditions of these rivers, it may be difficult to imagine that during the Trojan war they got furious and chased swift-footed Achilles in front of their waves. If the weather is clear, one can spot the grave mounds attributed to the heroes who fell during the same war*. Further off, in the form of two huge grey spots, the islands of Tenedos and Imbros can be distinguished, while when the sunlight falls at the right angle, in the further distance one can just make out the island of Samothrace, from whose *timbered* summit Poseidon watched the battle ground and encouraged the Achaeans. On the landward side, in the background rise the lofty pine-covered slopes of the Ida mountains, which accommodated Zeus when he came to look at the war.

In the valley where Achilles dragged the corpse of Hector behind his chariot, whence earlier Zeus abducted Ganymede, the son of Tros, the legendary founder of Troia, to serve his as his cup bearer on Mount Olympus, one can today see fertile fields of cotton, flocks of grazing sheep and Kumkale village. At present, the sea has retreated some 5 km away from the site. This particular geographic location, eminently suitable for agriculture, fishing, hunting and sea trade, explains why the same place has been continually settled since

*The highest one, which is easily spotted in the distance and towards the left, is attributed to Ajax.

Top Steatite mould. Troia VIIa (1275–1240 BC). Çanakkale Museum. On one side the mould contains the matrices for two ring-shaped pendants and three spherical beads. On the other, four ring-pendants and three slender segmented beads.

Centre Baked clay ceremonial vessel. Troia VI (1800–1275 BC). Çanakkale Archaeological Museum.

Bottom Baked clay stirrup jar. Troia VI (1800–1275 BC). Çanakkale Archaeological Museum

3000 BC.

The excavations carried out in the levels belonging Troia VI show that, during this period, the city had closer contacts with the Cyclades and mainland Greece, rather than with Anatolia. The type of baked clay pottery which is referred to as Grey Minyan Ware and made at a potter's wheel, coated, burnished, and decorated mostly with horizontal wavy lines – shapes imitating metal vessels such as bowls or without handles, jars of various sizes and some with trefoil mouths, other vessels with handles shaped in the form of animal heads all abundant in mainland Greece – and other painted baked clay pottery styles originating in Crete and Cyprus, all confirm the strong overseas ties and activities established during this period. Although few in number, the glittering gold, electrum, bronze and lead objects found in the levels of Troia VI again bring Homer to mind when he refers to the city throughout the *Iliad* as *rich in gold*.

This particular city of Troia, which is the focal point of the present day visitors to the site, is contemporary with Mycenae, Tirnys, Pylos, and other kingdoms in mainland Greece, as well as the Hittite Empire in Anatolia. The names in the *Iliad*, such as *Ahhiyawa*, *Alexandros*, *Ilios*, or *Troia**, and their counterparts in the Hittite texts, such as *Achaiwoi*, *Aleksandus*, *Wilios* or *Trausia*, are more frequent than might give the impression that they are accidental. When the inscribed tablets discovered at Hattuşaş in Boğazköy are deciphered, probably more information will be obtained about the relationship between the Trojans and the Hittites. The Tudhaliyas relief at Kemal Paşa near Izmır, and the Mother Goddess (Niobe) relief in Manisa, show that the power or the Hittites reached as far as the Aegean, and thus, their knowledge of the existence of a powerful kingdom in the Troas region would not be surprising. However, no Hittite object has yet been found in the excavations of Troia. The fact that the geography of the land between Troia and the Hittite capital made it unsuitable for trading, also that settlements established on the coast, such as Troia, preferred sea transportation, which was both safer and more convenient, must have played a role in this.

The cracks in the surviving fortifications, towers and walls of the houses of Troia VI and large blocks of stones fallen from these buildings, show that the city

* In the *Iliad* Homer often refers to Paris and Troia as *Alexandros* and *Ilios*, respectively.

must have suffered an earthquake. The absence of human skeletons further indicates that the earthquake must have taken place in stages and that people had enough time to run away and save themselves. These people, when the tremblings ceased, came back to Troia and built the level named VIIa by archaeologists. Their houses, which were small in size and many in number, together with the fact that they were built without being planned, indicate that they were erected in a short period of time. In other words, together with those who had escaped from the city and returned to it afterwards must have come other people, who had lived outside the city prior to the earthquake, but then felt the need to shelter within the city walls. In addition to this, the storage jars previously mentioned are further proof that the people of this period felt it necessary to store food long-term for the first time in the history of Troia. This new city lasted only thirty five years from 1275 BC to 1240 BC, and ended with a big fire. The skeletons and bones found under the fire debris indicate that the fire was accompanied by a massacre by an enemy. Archaeologists tend to believe that this weakened Troia VIIa was probably the one over which King Priam ruled.

The survivors rebuilt their city which is labelled by archaeologists as VIIb1, contuinued to live there until 1190 BC, however its heyday had gone forever, never to be regained.

After this important chapter in the history of Hisarlık tumulus was over, people of different stock seem to have settled there in about 1190 BC – while some of these newcomers continued their migration into the Anatolian interior – without any conflict being involved. This city is labelled VIIb2, and dates between 1190 BC and 1100 BC. During this period, the city walls were built with very large slabs (orthostats) forming their lower parts, and the houses, which were built standing side by side and independent from each other, contained numerous and doors. The former baked clay pottery was replaced by a new type shaped by hand rather than at the potter's wheel. This type of dark coloured, crude and primitive ware (buckelkeramik or knobbed ware) with fluting and knobs like horns is often encountered in south-eastern Europe. Research has shown that this culture lasted for there generations, and ended with another fire, leaving no trace. After this period, for a long time – during the Dark Age – until the 700s BC, nobody chose the tumulus as a place for settlement.

Marble pieces from the ceiling coffers of the temple of Athena. Troia IX (350 BC – 400 AD)

Marble pieces from the columns of the temple of Athena. Troia IX (350 BC – 400 AD)

Temple of Athena

Troia VIII (700–350 BC) & Troia IX (350 BC – 400 AD)

The Bronze Age buildings which must have stood at the top of the tumulus, must have been destroyed during the Hellenistic period, when this temple, its surrounding stoas and monumental gate building were constructed. In the course of time, the temple suffered the same history of destruction and perished as well. If something did survive, it was destroyed by the great trenches dug by Schliemann. The *Iliad* makes frequent references to a temple of Athena, such as in one of the early chapters where Hector, addressing his mother, says

'No, mother, you are the one to pray.
Go to Athena's shrine, the queen of plunder,
go with offerings, gather the older noble women
and take a robe, the largest, loveliest robe,
that you can find throughout the royal halls,
a gift that far and away you prize most yourself,
and spread it out across the sleek-haired
goddess' knees.
Then promise to sacrifice twelve heifers in her shrine,
yearlings never broken, if only she'll pity Troy,'

Such references together with Homer's statement about the position of the temple *on the summit of the city* have made archaeologists look for a temple of antiquity here, but with no result. The large marble ceiling coffer pieces, fluted column bases and capitals, give the visitors some idea about the dimensions of this Hellenistic and Roman edifice. It is known that it was constructed in Doric order and that Alexander the Great (336–323 BC), and later his general Lysimachus (323–281 BC) made generous contributions to it. During the Roman period it was enlarged and surrounded by columned sacred enclosures.

In 1865, when Frank Calvert made trial diggings in this area, samples of various Bronze Age settlement levels that he found under marble pieces belonging to the temple made him believe that the tumulus of Hisarlık was the actual site of Troia of Homer. The honour of digging and proving this, however, went to Schliemann. The temple was the most important monument of Troia during its last period, and famous visitors to the city at that time never missed the opportunity of visiting it, sacrificing, and dedicating gifts to the goddess sometimes in memory of the heroes who fell during the Trojan war.

Northeast tower (water tower) and cistern

Troia VI (1800–1275 BC)

This tower which was built around the most important water supply of the city – a well measuring 4 sq m wide and 8 m deep and hewn into the living rock and reaching the spring – is one of most impressive ruins of Troia VI. Its height and strength can be appreciated better from the valley. The narrow staircase which descends steeply from this tower is Hellenistic.

Great theatre

Troia IX (350 BC – 400 AD)

On the right, looking northeast, those with sharp eyes can make out the ruins of the great theatre which is claimed to have once held 10,000 spectators, and which commanded a view of both sea and valley. The slope where the rows of seats of the cavea were set has not yet been dug. During his excavations, Carl Blegen uncovered what is left of the orchestra and stage building, and found decorated marble pieces.

From this high point of the present tumulus, one descends to the lower ground, where large marble blocks belonging to the temple of Athena are scattered here and there. This is also the place where one will see the remains of the earliest settlement on the site, Troia I*.

* In this area which was used by both Troia I and Troia II the ruins of both settlements are intermingled and rather confusing. In this guide book it has been preferred to describe Troia I first, and then Troia II.

Great theatre. Troia IX (350 BC – 400 AD)

Northeast tower of Troia VI (1800–1275 BC) and the Hellenistic stairs

Great theatre. Ruins of the orchestra. Troia IX (350 BC – 400 AD)

Fortification wall. Troia I (3000–2500 BC). The large stone blocks at the top belong to Troia IX (350–400 AD).

Fortification walls, tower and megaron houses

Troia I (3000–2500 BC)

Excavations have brought to light the fact that the earliest of the nine cities of Troia founded during the Early Bronze Age on rock ground, which was 16 m above the plain*.

Trial diggings carried out in the alluvial plain extending in front of the tumulus have shown that, at the time when the first settlers came here, a shallow bay existed. In other words, these earliest settlers of Troia lived virtually on the coast. This first settlement was a small fortress-like village and a piece of its wall made of rough unworked stones can be distinguished above the slope on the left, resting under a few rows or large sandstone blocks which belong to the temple of Athena of Troia IX.

Troia I had a diameter of approximately 90 m, and was surrounded by a wall with two gates. Archaeologists have divided this settlement into ten levels and decided that during this uninterrupted period the height of the tumulus increased by more than 4 m. The piece of wall already seen and other remains soon

* Starting from this date, for more than 3000 years, settlements were to be built on top each other, and the height of the tumulus increased. From the fact that the height of the tumulus was about 32 m when archaeologists started digging, it can be concluded that during this 3000 year period the height of the tumulus increased by another 16 m.

to be seen are in a better state of preservation and belong to the latest period of this early history.

The main entrance to the city was on the south side*. This entrance was 3 m wide and shaped like a corridor. On both sides it was flanked by towers. The remains of the east tower, which has survived, reach to the height of 3.5 m at present. Its base is made of fairly large stones which become smaller and distinctly narrower as it goes higher. Adjoining this tower is a piece of the city wall which slopes in towards the top. It shows strong and sturdy workmanship of unworked stone plastered together with clay mortar at the bottom. settlement this direction would be crossfired from the towers. Blegen's excavation team have been able to trace the fortifications for about 115 m by digging tunnels and wells.

This Early Bronze Age settlement is contemporary with similar civilizations such as Iassos (Güllük) or Old Smyrna (Bayraklı) in Western Anatolia. Like them it was founded at a place eminently suitable for hunting, fishing and agriculture, during a period when trade may have been weak, and at the same time it was fairly impregnable against attack. Although there is

* From this period on, all the nine cities of Troia were to have their main entrances on the landward side, looking in the same direction.

East tower of the south gate. Troia II (2500–2200 BC)

no information about the origins and language of these early settlers they are regarded as autonomous products of Anatolia, and were probably ruled by somebody from the native population. In the course of time, these native rulers would accumulate wealth through the production of olive oil, wheat and wine; and their role as rulers would become hereditary, passing from father to son.

Archaeological finds indicate that during this period the potter's wheel was unknown and pottery was shaped by hand. The monochrome grey and black burnished baked clay pottery sherds discovered show that vessels with lids or handles, mostly jugs with projecting spouts like beaks, and various bowls with shapes suitable for everyday use, were in favour. Stones which must have been used for pounding or for grinding wheat suggest an agricultural lifestyle. Weapons were made from hard stones such as obsidian or flint, or from raw copper or lead. Articles made from animal bones or horns are also encountered. Spindle whorls, loom weights, and bone and copper needles of various sizes indicate that these people were familiar with weaving. The major food sources included cattle, goats, sheep and pigs, fish and sea molluscs; also rabbits and deer to a lesser degree. Wheat appears towards the end of this era. Stone beads and ornaments, bone and stone idols, and the decoration encountered on baked clay pottery, appear to have been their only contact with plastic art. The limestone relief in the shape of a human face, found by Blegen, is regarded as being the oldest example of sculpture encountered in the area so far. Although a cemetery has not been discovered, from time to time children's skeletons are found buried under the floors of the houses, with or without urns.

Research has shown that during this period people lived in fairly large houses, built separately and shaped in a long narrow rectangles. The entrance often had a long narrow forecourt, obtained by projecting side walls. The walls were made of sun-dried mudbricks containing straw and resting on stone foundation. They were bound together by a thinner sort of clay and plastered. The floors were covered with beaten clay. Roofs were made of horizontal wooden beams covered with mud and branches on top of these. It seems that when these dwellings were destroyed, whether by fire, storm, earthquake, or the enemy, people preferred not to clear the debris away, but smoothed simply over the area — debris and all —

Limestone stele (in secondary use) decorated with a human face. Troia I (3000–2500 BC). İstanbul Archaeological Museums

Spindle whorls. Troia I (3000–2500 BC). Troia II (2500–2200 BC), Troia III (2200–2050 BC) and Troia VI (1800–1275 BC). Çanakkale Archaeological Museum

Baked clay vessel. Troia I (3000–2500 BC). Çanakkale Archaeological Museum.

Megaron houses. Troia I (3000–2500 BC) (view from south)

Megaron houses 102 and 103. Troia I (3000–2500 BC) (view from west)

and built on top of it.

This simple type of house plan, known as the megaron, later became widespread and was used all over the Aegean world, eventually coming to be used as a prototype of temple architecture. The most common feature of these houses was the existence of a hearth situated in the centre of the room. The remains of some of these houses can be seen today standing in a row side by side, at the bottom of the trench of Schliemann. The brick wall which runs along the eastern border of these houses is modern but built in the same manner and with the same material that people used 5000 years ago. While in the future it was to give archaeologists an idea about the durability of Bronze Age sun-dried mudbrick walls, it also prevents the slope above it from falling down. Among these houses the one labelled as 102 – situated somewhat away from the visitor's view in Schliemann's trench – has a rectangular plan and dimensions of 18.5 x 7 metres. Both of its side walls are extended in the front to create a sort of porch. It had a hearth at the centre and another one close to the eastern wall. The two platforms adjoining the walls probably served as seats or beds. In the eastern corner, a shallow pit was used for storing food; animal bones and sea-shells discovered here show that food was eaten in this corner. During the diggings two separate children's graves were encountered under the floor of the room. The children skeletons – altogether six in number – encountered in the same manner indicate the high percentage of death among newly born babies. Archaeologists believe that the history of Troia I ended with a fire.

Clay model of the megaron houses 102 and 103. Troia I (3000–2500 BC). İstanbul Archaeological Museums

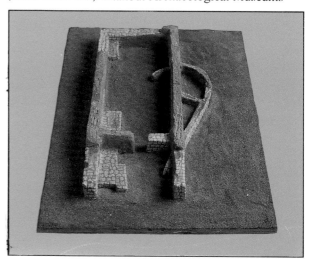

South fortification wall. Troia II (2500–2200 BC)

Monumental gate, megaron palace, ramp and fortification walls

Troia II (2500–2200 BC)

Research has shown that culturally Troia I and Troia II, the second settlement built after levelling the ruins of the previous one, did not differ. The second city covered a larger area, its diameter having increased to 110 m. This city had a precise plan, rarely encountered in other settlements of the Early Bronze Age. Archaeologists discovered that during the seven layers of this city the height of the tumulus increased by about 3 m, and it was expanded towards the south.

Among the baked clay pottery encountered in Troia II, in additon to that shaped by hand, samples shaped at the potter's wheel are encountered. The morphology of pottery has become richer comprising new forms such as tall drinking goblets with two large handles and a round base, named *depas amphikypellon* by Schliemann after Homer, and new relief decorations on lids and jugs representing human faces. Pounding or grinding stones and decorated spindle whorls are numerous. The expanding yarn and weaving industry is confirmed by the high number of sheep and goat bones. Beans, lentils and wheat are known to have been added to the already existing food sources such as domestic animals and seafood. The use of metals has become more widespread. In addition to arsenical bronze, bronze from the alloy of copper and tin, and copper was produced. The Trojans of this period probably utilized metal scissors to shear their sheep and did not have to pluck them with their hands as their Mesopotamian counterparts did. The Trojan rulers must have accumulated enough wealth to attract

Plan of Troia II (2500–2200 BC) during the last period of its history

Clay model of Troia II (2500–2200 BC) displayed at the entrance of present ruins of Troia and İstanbul Archaeological Museums

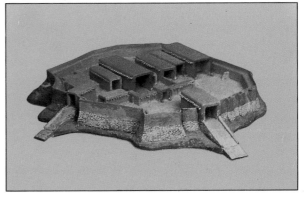

Baked clay jar with three handles. Troia II (2500–2200 BC). Çanakkale Archaeological Museum

Baked clay goblet with two handles (*depas amphikypellon*). Troia II (2500–2200 BC). Çanakkale Archaeological Museum

itinerant potters, artisans and skilled metalsmiths who could produce good filigree jewellery for them. The best example of the material culture of the Trojan rulers of this period is the treasury that Schliemann discovered. Gold, electrum, copper and bronze articles found in this hoarde indicate the existence of a very high level of life which utilized a high standard of metalwork, bringing to mind the riches discovered in the royal graves at Alacahöyük near Hattushash.

The jewellery, weapons and other artefacts brought to light at these settlements of antiquity show that during this period Anatolia had very skillful metalworkers who probably offered their services to rulers of different cultures, travelling from one region to the other. Among the metals they utilized are gold, silver, electrum, iron, lead and copper – all found in Anatolia – and tin, which is thought to have been brought from the Zagros mountains, the Iberic peninsula or Britain – unless an undiscovered Bronze Age tin source existed in Anatolia. The surviving jewellery from this period shows that these metalworkers were experienced in shaping the gold by moulding or by hammering and beating; and enriching their work with granulation, filigree and other techniques and occasionally enamelling. Among the

stones used are: obsidian, meerschaum, jasper, cornelian and nephrite, and locally produced faience is encountered.

The fact that all such articles belonging to Troia II were discovered under about one metre of fire debris, indicates that the city was destroyed by a great and sudden conflagration without any apparent involvement of any outside enemy. The treasury he discovered, the city's destruction by fire, and his haste, made Schliemann believe that Troia II, which he named the Burned City, was the Troia of Homer.

Even though the remains of Troia II – apart from the ramp and its adjoining walls – are not impressive, they give archaeologists enough information about the architecture of the city. It is known that its main gate was in the south as it was in the previous city. The monumental gate on this side, which had the appearance of a long narrow passage, was succeeded by a courtyard with a smooth pebbled floor built during the latest period of the city's history. In order to reach the king's palace it was necessary to pass through a second gateway and a similar courtyard. A stone base found in this sector of the ruins has made archaeologists think that this gateway was probably built like a columned portico, and in addition to its nice architecture, it provided shade in the heat of the summer. At the other side of the second courtyard stood the king's palace, a large megaron building of two floors, with a length of 35–40 m and a width of 13 m including the walls – the thickness of each wall measuring 1.5 m. At its centre there was a raised circular platform with a hearth.

Most of this building was destroyed by Schliemann's trench but the surviving parts of its long walls show sun-dried mudbrick construction resting on stone foundations. Almost all the gold and electrum articles discovered during excavations have been found in and around the area occupied by this large building. This house was flanked by smaller houses with the same plan. The westernmost building was divided into smaller rooms and was probably used as a magazine for weapons. These megarons were planned parallel to each other and also had mudbrick walls constructed using clay mortar and reinforced by horizontal and perpendicular beams. The walls were plastered with a thick layer of clay on their souter and inner surfaces and the floors were made of beaten clay.

To the southeast of the second courtyard stood a second monumental gate which opened to a stone-paved ramp 21 m long and 7.5 m wide. This ramp and the adjoining city walls on both sides are the most impressive ruins that have survived from Troia II. At the point where the ramp and the 5.25 m-wide entrance meet, there stood a wooden door of two leaves strengthened with copper and bronze pieces. The city walls are constructed from stone blocks with smoothed outer faces, sloping in towards the top. Their upper parts were probably made of sun-dried mudbricks reinforced with wooden beams. Both the stone and brick sections of the walls were covered with a thick layer of plaster which did not survive to the present day. The discovery of the riches known as the Treasure of Troia, or the Jewels of Helen, at the foot of the walls on the left, has given to this spot a particular mystery and significance for visitors to Troia*.

Climbing the steep path opposite the ramp, on the right, one comes across the poor remains of two megaron buildings which are known as VIA and VIB, both belonging to Troia VI. The samples of Mycenaean pottery that Schliemann found here helped him to

*After a long period of time, Schliemann was to reluctantly give up his conviction that the treasury he discovered did not belonged to Troia of Homer, but in fact came from an earlier city.

Remains of the south gate. Troia II (2500–2200 BC)

Arsenical bronze axes and agricultural implements. Troia II (2500–2200 BC). Çanakkale Archaeological Museum

Stone and animal bone idols. Troia II (2500–2200 BC). Çanakkale Archaeological Museum

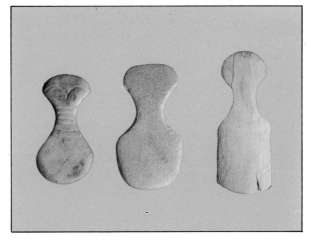

believe that the ruins where he discovered the treasury did indeed belong to Troia of Homer, which must have had close contacts with that city and consequently utilized Mycenaean baked clay vessels. Even a causal visitor, however, may notice that these ruins are at a much higher level than the ruins where Schliemann discovered the treasury and also quite a distance outside the fortification walls. Later, in 1890, Blegen and Dörpfeld unearthing more Mycenaean baked clay vessels here reconfirmed that buildings belonged to Troia VI.

In the second book of the *Aeneid*, Aeneas recounts the tale of the wooden horse to Queen Dido of Carthage:

Top left Model sun-dried mudbrick wall on original stone foundation. Megaron palace. Troia II (2500–2200 BC)

Top right Ramp at the southwest entrance of Troia II and the west fortification wall. The so-called 'Treasure of Priam' was found by Schliemann at the bottom of the wall extending to the north.

Bottom left Stonework of the fortification wall. Troia II (2500–2200 BC)

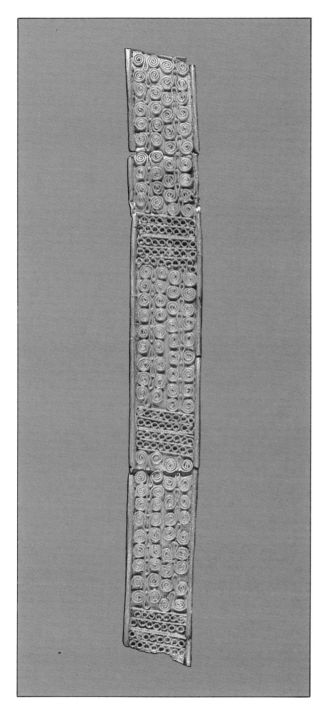

Gold bracelet. Troia II (2500–2200 BC). İstanbul Archaeological Museums. This 23 carat gold bracelet was found in an earthenware pot in the megaron palace by Schliemann in 1878, and is thought to have belonged to a wealthy lady. Its surface is decorated with small rings and double spirals, a motif which appears throughout the Near East during this period. The spiral groups are soldered to the hammered body of the bracelet and separated from each other by rows of tiny rings. The edges are framed from thick gold plate strengthened by silver wire folded over them.

Gold pendant headgear. Troia II (2500–2200 BC). İstanbul Archaeological Museums. The uppermost parts of this gold headgear – also found by Schliemann – are made of twenty three wires twisted into the shape of a basket. Below each is a group of four horizontal plates with vertical grooves on the front. From the hooks attached to the plates hung chains, composed of small rings, and bearing leaves – those at the end of each chain being larger. The veins of the leaves are indicated by vertical raised lines.

The Greeks grew weary of the tedios war,
And by Minerva's aid, a fabric reard,
Which like a steed of monstrous height appeared:
The sides were planked with pine: they feigned it made
For their return, and this the vow they paid.
Thus they pretend; but in the hollow side,
Selected numbers of their soldiers hide:
With inward arms the dire machine they load;
And iron bowels stuff the dark abode.
In sight of Troy lies Tenedos, an isle
(While Fortune did on Priam's empire smile)
Renowned for wealth; but since, a faithless bay,
Where ships exposed to wind and weather lay.
There was their Fleet concealed.
We thought, for Greece
Their sails were hoisted, and our fears release.
The Trojans, cooped within their walls so long,
Unbar their gates, and issue in a throng

...

And had not Heaven the fall of Troy designed,
Or had not men been fated to be blind,
Enought was said and don't inspire a better mind.
Then had our lances pierced the treacherous wood,
And Ilian towers and Priam's empire stood.

Opposite Trojan horse. Illustration from the late fifteenth century manuscript of Raoul Lefèvre's French version of the medieval story of the Trojan war. The hatch of the wooden horse is open and a ladder is ready for the descent of the Achaeans represented inside. While the horse is shown standing at a breach in the walls beside a gate named as La Porte Dardane or the Dardanian Gate, in the background the Achaeans have already started butchering the inhabitants in La Ville de Troia, or the City of Troia.

Trojan Horse. Detail from the representation on the neck of a relief pithos. *c* 675 BC. Mykonos Museum, Greece. Each hatch shows the wide-eyed head of an Achaean warrior. The armed warriors outside may be the Achaeans who have already climbed out of the horse or the Trojans advancing to resist the Achaeans above.

Trojan horse. Illustration by Jean Mielon in a medieval manuscript of Christine de Pisan's *Letter of Othea to Hector*. A nonwooden conception of the Trojan horse is shown being pushed through the walls by figures clothed as in all medieval representations.

If the details are summarized, archaeologists tend to believe that Troia II was destroyed by a fire so big that the rich ruling class fled leaving their valuables behind. Similar catastrophes occurring at varios sites of antiquity in mainland Greece, and the decline in material culture that followed, are thought to have resulted from the Indo-European incursions which started in Central Europe towards the beginning of second millenium BC. Nevertheless, the archaeological finds give no sign of any intrusive element from Europe. This fact and the successive settlements of Troia III, Troia IV and Troia V show that the Indo-European destroyers of Troia II did not settle here but continued their migration. Although the unscientific manner in which Heinrich Schliemann dug the tumulus did not leave anything from these three unimportant epochs, in order not to leave any chronological gap between the first and the last cities of Troia, it is necessary to say a few words about these settlements as well.

West gate VIM of Troia VI (1800–1275 BC) by which the wooden horse is thought to have been carried into the city

West gate VIU
Troia VI (1800–1275 BC)

At this point, the visitor is very close to one of the west gates of Troia VI named by archaeologists as VIU and through which the wooden horse is thought to have been dragged into the city – on tree trunks. It falls to the side of the visitor's path. The piece of construction which blocks the gate is half thick of the original fortification wall of Troia VI and it is not founded on bedrock. The colour, workmanship and the irregular size of the stones used here, all differing from the typical stonework of Troia VI, have made archaeologists conclude that this gate must have been rebuilt in haste after it was demolished*.

* This information can be better appreciated when one reaches the northwestern corner of the sacred precinct from where the blocked up gate can be viewed.

Troia III (2200–2050 BC)

During the history of this city, which constitutes the third Early Bronze Age era of it, life changed very little. Research has shown that during the four separate settlement levels, the height of the tumulus increased by about 3 more m. At this time although the walls of houses were built in the same manner, and had beaten clay floors similar to the houses of the previous cities, individual dwellings are not encountered. The buildings were separated by very narrow streets. One distinct architectural feature of this city is that the fortification walls were built entirely of stone, i.e. without the sun-dried mudbrick superstructure.

Archaeological finds give the impression that no important changes occurred regarding food sources and that similar conditions to those of the previous period also prevailed in pottery and weaving.

Baked clay ceremonial vessel. Troia II (2200–2050 BC) or Troia IV? (2050–1900 BC). İstanbul Archaeological Museums. The vessel is handmade and assumed to represent the Mother Goddess. The female body is also the body of the vessel. The mouth is at the top of her head, and the spout is a kantharos held at its handles by the thin arms emerging from the neck. There are two conical projections with holes on the chest for breasts. The neck is adorned with a necklace in relief. The handle of the vessel is at the back of her head.

Baked clay ceremonial vessel. Troia III (2200–2050 BC) or Troia IV? (2050–1900 BC). İstanbul Archaeological Museums

Troia IV (2050–1900 BC)

This city, which was made of five separate settlement layers, was the last Early Bronze Age settlement of Troia. Objects brought to light in excavations show that, during this period, relations with the Aegean world the Near East and Central Anatolia – probably through the Aegean and Mediterranean routes – increased. Houses were built side by side but not independent of each other, with walls made of sun-dried mudbrick plastered with a thin layer of mud or clay on stone foundations, and has one or two rooms with beaten clay floors. The entrances of the houses opened all onto the same street. For the first time in Troia, domed ovens appeared, built in courtyards. Weaving seems to have continued along the previous lines and sea turtles are encountered for the first time as part of the diet. The practice of building city walls entirely of stone which applied to Troia III seem to have continued during Troia IV as well.

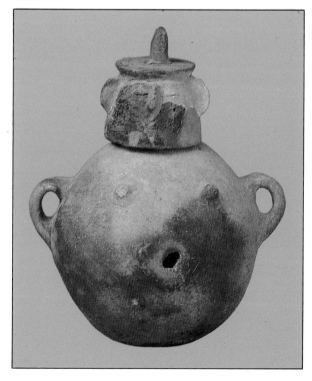

Troia V (1900–1800 BC)

This city of six settlement levels totalling 2 m altogether, falls into the transition period from the Early Bronze Age to the Middle Bronze Age in western Anatolia. The archaeological finds show that connections with Cyprus had by now been added to foreign commercial ties. Fortifications, which bore saw-like projections, were built of unworked stones at the bottom and with sun-dried mudbrick superstructure. A development is also observed in city planning. Small rooms built on there sides of a rectangular courtyard, containing platfoms for sitting or sleeping, and domed or beehive-shaped ovens, are also observed. Under the floor of one the houses, the skeleton of a newly born baby in foetal position was found.

During this period, while cloth weaving continued, hunting decreased and the consumption of cattle and pork meat increased. As a result of the more widespread use of the fast turning potter's wheel, the shape of baked clay vessels became more symmetrical and some of these bear white decorations recalling crosses.

VIM building. Troia VI (1800–1275 BC)

VIM building

Troia VI (1800–1275 BC)

As one continues walking towards the sacred precinct, the most interesting ruin is an L shaped construction which is made of large rectangular porous limestone blocks with strong stonework, both features being typical of the fortifications of Troia VI. In the corners larger blocks were used. The 27 m-long wall is divided vertically into five sections with perpendicular shallow offsets similar to those already observed on the east wall of Troia VI. This building has two small rooms on the western side, and a large room of 5 x 3 m. The small rooms are thought to have been used for storage. Archaeologists have noticed that the northern corner of the large room was used for cooking and eating. The six storage jars discovered buried into the ground along the western wall of the large room show that the building must have been used during the Troia VIIa period, which succeeded the earthquake of Troia VI*. The enormous size of this originally two-storeyed

VIM building. Troia VI (1800–1275 BC) (view from west)

* A careful visitor may spot some of the cracks caused by the previously mentioned earthquake, passing vertically through the large stone pieces close to the edge where the two walls join each other.

VIM building. Wall with the vertical offsets and earthquake cracks. Troia VI (1800–1275 BC)

Baked clay glaux (owl-cup). c 450–440 BC. Troia VIII. Çanakkale Archaeological Museum. The vessel is decorated with an owl represented between olive sprays.

Baked clay censer. Troia VIII (700–350 BC). Çanakkale Archaeological Museum

Baked clay aryballos. Troia VIII (700–350 BC). Çanakkale Archaeological Museum. The vessel which must have been used as a perfume or oil container is decorated with warriors bearing helmets and large round shields.

structure, and its commanding position over the plain where the battle was fought, give the impression that it must have served as a kind of palace.

Troia VIII (700–350 BC)

When one leaves the actual city of Troia VI through an opening in its walls, sightseeing still continues on the soil of Troia VIII, which occupied a much larger area than the previous city.

After Troia VIIb2 (1190–1100 BC) no settlement was made on the tumulus for a long time. Towards the end of the ninth century BC, new migration, which is assumed to have started from the Aegean world colonized Troia at the same time as other settlements such as Bisanthe or Rhaedestus (Tekirdağ), Nicomedia (İzmit) and Byzantium (İstanbul). Troia was colonized by Greek settlers around 700 BC. This new settlement was a small town called 'Ilion', and remained as a nodest settlement until it became a part of the Roman Empire and it was built on the ruins of previous cities, making use of their architectural materials. Its population is assumed to have been around 3000 inhabitants. The results of excavations are not adequate enough to give a clear picture of the architecture of this era. Nevertheless, houses with a rectangular plan, a door in any wall, and sometimes with a hearth, were used. Circular areas which were paved with stone and must have served to dry figs, grapes or similar items, are encountered. Written documents mention an archaic temple of Athena of this period, of which no trace has been found.

Samples of Corinthian, Eastern Greek, Attic and Ionian baked clay pottery dating from this period bear witness to close cultural and commercial contacts with the Aegean world. Among the other objects discovered are: spindle whorls and loom weights, bronze needles (fibulae) used to stitch clothing, bone or stone idols and other kinds of baked clay vessels.

Sacred precinct

After examining the surviving part of the VIM building of Troia VI and walking out through the western walls of the same period, immediately to the right and in the west, on lower ground, one comes across the sacred precinct.

Although no information has been obtained about the deities worshipped here, one of the earliest must have been the Anatolian gooddess Cybele, and it is assumed that the same piece of ground had been used as a sacred place probably since the foundation of the earliest settlement.

Among the surviving ruins of the sacred precinct, whose entrance was in the northwestern corner, the largest belong to the Hellenistic Age. The high altar is assumed to have been built towards the end of the fourth century BC; its marble stairs and revetments are Roman. Of the Hellenistic 'rustica' wall, constructed from regularly cut limestone blocks, a large section has survived to the present in good state of preservation. The Hellenistic sacrificial altar at the centre, on the lower ground, has made use of a pre-Hellenistic pit used as an altar, and is connected to the nearby well by a channel for disposing of blood and dirty water. The large well must have supplied the pure water required before the actual sacrifice.

Sacred precinct. Detail from the Hellenistic wall. The wall at the back belongs to Troia VI (1800–1275 BC)

Sacred precinct

Marble pieces belonging to Troia IX (350 BC – 400 AD)

Troia IX (350 BC – 400 AD)

Although culturally this city was closely related to the previous one, it covered a very much larger area. In 85 BC, the Roman general Gaius Flavius Fimbria sacked Troia and – it is said – afterwards boasted thad he had done in eleven days what Achaeans took took ten years to accomplish. The Trojans responded that they had not had any Hector to defend the city. Since Roman rulers regarded their ancestry as having descended from Aeneas, who was the cousin of Hector, and fled after the city was sacked, they supported Troia, and the city gained new momentum especially during the reigns of Julius Caesar (59–44 BC) who claimed descent from Aeneas, mother Venus and Octavius Augustus (31 BC – 14 AD). During this period, the city – Novum Ilium – was surrounded by a fortification wall which extended for about 3.5 km. The temple of Athena was restored, and the area it covered , including its sacred enclosures was about 9.500 sq m. In the later part of the city's history, the Roman emperor Constantine the Great (324–337 AD) considered founding the new capital of his empire hereabouts. Obviously, however, he eventually decided on Byzantium.

As one continues sightseeing, it gradually becomes clear that some of the most important monuments of Troia IX must have stood on the two sides of a main street extending in an east west direction in this area.

Baked clay figurine (Cybele?). Hellenistic. Sofular.
Çanakkale Archaeological Museum

Baked clay figurine. Hellenistic. Assos. Çanakkale
Archaeological Museum

Baked clay female figurine. Troia IX (350 BC – 400 AD).
Çanakkale Archaeological Museum

Marble relief of Heracles. (First century BC – First century
AD. Troia IX (350 BC – 400 AD). İstanbul Archaeological
Museums

Marble pieces belonging to Troia IX (350 BC – 400 AD)

Nymphaeum (monumental fountain)

Troia IX (350 BC – 400 AD)

On the right, looking towards the fields to the south, are the ruins of a nymphaeum or monumental fountain, which belonged to a gymnasium (palestra) complex. Here archaeologists have spotted mosaic pavements decorated with human and animal figures. In the same direction a burial ground which is thought to have been used during the last period of Troia VI was spotted and remains of cremated bodies placed in jars which were covered with a lid and stood upright often just a few cm below the surface of the ground were unearthed. The funeral gifts they contained were mostly beads, bronze pins and rings, and small pottery items.

Nymphaeum (monumental fountain). Troia IX (350 BC – 400 AD)

Little theatre

Troia IX (350 BC – 400 AD)

This little building on the left-hand side towards north known as the little theatre or odeon is today probably the best preserved and most attractive ruin, dating from the Roman era of Troia. Although the stage building has not survived, its orchestra and the seats for spectators have still retained their marble revetments in places. The building was probably covered with a wooden roof.

Little theatre. South-west entrance. Troia IX (350 BC – 400 AD)

Little theatre. Troia IX (350 BC – 400 AD)

South gate (Scaean Gates?). Troia VI (1800–1275 BC)

South gate

Troia VI (1800–1275 BC)

This gate is thought by Schliemann to be the *Scaean Gates* of Homeric Troia, the main gate of the city by which the Trojan heroes left the city and went to fight on the battlefield. It was protected on its left side by the *Great Tower* which is referred to by Homer as thus

The old men of the realm held seats above the gates. Long years had brought their fighting days to a halt but they were eloquent speakers still, clear as cicadas settled on treetops, lifting their voices through the forest, rising softly, failing, dying away... So they waited, the old chiefs of Troy, as they sat aloft the tower. And catching sight of Helen moving along the ramparts, they murmured one to another, gentle, winged words:

In the *Iliad*, Helen introduces the Achaean heroes that she could recognise to King Priam from a high structure such as this, from which the battlefield could be observed.

Helen the child of Zeus replied,
That's Laertes' son, the great tactician Odysseus.
He was bred in the land of Ithaca, rocky ground

and he's quick at every treachery under the sun—the man of twists and turns.
...
Why, that's the giant Ajax, bulwark of the Achaeans. And Idomeneus over there–standing with his Cretans–like a god, you see? And the Cretan captains
...
Castor breaker of horses and the hardy boxer Polydeuces.

The upright monolithic stones like menhirs originally six in number – placed in front of the left side of the gate are thought to have carried a religious connotation, probably related to the ceremonies carried out here on entering or leaving the city. Their strong foundations, worn surfaces and shortened height show that they have stood here for a very long period of time. Originally, when a Trojan entered the city by this gate, he could walk up to the acropolis following the wide street which also had a channel for sewage running underneath it in the centre. It is assumed that Troia VI was split into large sectors by such wide streets which came together at the great open courtyard at the top of the acropolis, in front of the king's palace, and on the terraces going up towards the acropolis independent megaron buildings were constructed.

The Pillar house

Troia VI (1800–1275 BC)

The name of the building comes from the pillar standing at its centre. These ruins of a large megaron, measuring 26 x 12 m, are the most extensive among the remains of dwellings, and this building is thought to have been in use during both Troia VI and Troia VIIa. Its shape, becoming larger towards the rear, with a porch, a central large room and three small rooms at the back on the west side, can easily be distinguished.

It is thought that food was cooked in the western corner of the large room and the small rooms on this side served to store food. While one of the pyramidal stone pillars which supported the roof has partially survived, only a small fragment of the second pillar has been found. The existence of its entrance in the north wall of the large room distinguishes this building from a typical megaron.

Pillar house. Troia VI (1800–1275 BC)

Surviving part of the 'pillar' of the pillar house. Troia VI (1800–1275 BC)

Pillar house. Entrance in the west wall

The ruin of the house situated immediately to the rear of this building to the northeast – known as house 630 – is interesting because it shows a sample of the stonework of the early period of Troia VI and has a different plan. Its walls are built from small stones, and the building dates from the eighteenth century BC. Its floor and the small column base have been brought to light during excavations.

House 630. *c* 1700 BC.

Gate tower (Great Tower of Ilios?). South gate. Troia VI (1800–1275 BC)

Upright stone blocks. South gate

Bouleterion (council house). Troia IX (350 BC – 400 AD)

Bouleterion (council house)

Troia IX (350 BC – 400 AD)

The last ruin to be seen before leaving the ruins of Troia are those of a small amphitheatre, which is thought to have served as a council house or even as an odeon. Its plan consists of a council of a rectangular entrance, an orchestra in the shape of a half circle, and a sloping cavea where spectators seats were situated. The large marble pieces on the floor of its entrance rest on the wall of Troia VI that was built approximately fifteen hundred years earlier.

A large part of the left side of the council house was built on a building which belonged to Troia VI and is named by archaeologists as the 'anta house' owing to the surviving part of one of its antae, or plasters, slightly projecting from its lateral walls.

The discovery of plenty of burnt animal bones but nothing else in this ruin have led the archaeologists to think that the room was probably used for sacrifices during the religious ceremonies held at the south gate.

The actual sightseeing tour of the ancient ruins of Troia comes to an end at this point. The excavations of the later period of its history are far from being complete yet. The granite column pieces scattered in among the old oak trees on the right and towards the south are thought to have come from the agora which occupied this area. The rest of the ruins of Troia IX extend under the fields to the south, in the direction of the village of Kalafat. A careful visitor, however, will probably notice that some of these started on both sides of the street immediately after the ticket office to the east when entering into the site.

Heinrich Schliemann (1822–1890)

Sophia Schliemann wearing the so-called 'Jewels of Helen'. The photograph became one of the most popular portraits of the nineteenth century. Schliemann describes the headgear found in a silver vase thus: *The one diadem consists of a gold fillet... from which there hang on either side seven little chains to cover the temples, each of which has eleven square leaves with a groove; these chains are joined to one another by four little cross chains, at the end of which hangs a glittering golden idol of the tutelar goddess of Troy...*

DISCOVERY OF TROIA, HEINRICH SCHLIEMANN and THE TREASURE

The first excavations, although very limited, are known to have been carried out at Troia by Frank Calvert, who acted as both American and British Consul at Çanakale during the second half of the nineteenth century. In 1865, he ventured trial diggings in the part of the tumulus which he actually owned, and upon coming across samples of different layers of settlements under the Hellenistic and Roman ruins, thought that Hisarlık was probably the site of Homeric Troia, the city of the Bronze Age. However, since he had overcharged his government for the food he sold to the navy during the Crimean War – thus accumulating immense wealth – he was very unpopular with London, and his request for funds and help evoked no response. Afterwards, when he took Schliemann around the site and showed him the results of his diggings, the latter was immediately convinced, mostly because of the geographical position of the tumulus which exactly fitted into Homer's description, that this was indeed the original site of Homeric Troia.

The innumerable travel notes, articles, letters and books Heinrich Schliemann (1822–1890) left behind recount a very colourful life story, in which his actual life and discoveries, reality and dreams, became inseparable from each other. The arguments about his personality and discoveries began even while he lived, and did not cease even after his death.

Schliemann was born on January sixth, 1822 in Mecklenburg, Germany as the son of a pastor. In *Ilios*, which he wrote later, he claims that he owed his first encounter with Troia, when he was 8 years old, to the *Universal History* of Jerrer that he received from his father as a Christmas present. Schliemann says that when he saw the picture of Aeneas fleeing away from Troia, and running between the burning towers, he decided to excavate Troia.

> *'Father, Jerrer must have seen Troy,' (Schliemann says he said) 'otherwise he could not have represented it here.'*
>
> *'My son,' he replied, 'that is merely a fanciful picture'...*
>
> *'Father!' retorted I, 'if such walls once existed they cannot have been completely destroyed: vast ruins of them must still remain, but hidden away beneath the dust of ages'...*
>
> *In the end we both agreed that I should one day excavate Troy'.*

Schliemann, at the age of 19, settled in Amsterdam and started working as a clerk with a company dealing in indigo, olive oil and the tea trade. During this period he was to begin teaching himself English, French and Spanish, to which he would later add a number of languages, including Greek and Arabic. After learning Russian, he was sent to St Petersburg where, after a short while, he became self-employed, made his first fortune in the indigo trade, and became a Russian citizen. In 1850, he moved to America and during the Gold Rush in California, he made his second fortune in banking. After two years he was back in Russia at the time of the Crimean War, making a third fortune by selling potassium nitrate to the Russian army, which was indispensable for the production of black powder.

The commercial ethics of Schliemann have often been the subject of argument, and he was frequently accused of being dishonest in some of his business dealings. Meanwhile he had married and had three children. In 1869 he moved to New York, became an American citizen – Henry Schliemann – and got a divorce.

In his memoires, he also mentions that during this period he decided to terminate his business life and spend most of his time on more intellectual pursuits, which included buying land in the States and working in the agricultural sector, and becoming a scientist, probably a philologist. Such confessions give the impression that, even if he had planned it before, his real interest in archaeology started with Troia – an unfortunate event for this site – when, in the summer of 1868, he met Frank Calvert and visited the Troas region. The latter was a wealthy intellectual Englishman who had cultivated hobbies similar to those of Schliemann and he allowed Schliemann to dig in his part of the tumulus of Hisarlık.

It should probably be remembered that, during this period, nobody but Frank Calvert and Schliemann believed that this tumulus could be the actual site of Homeric Troia. Although the *Iliad* was regarded in the second half of the nineteenth century as a most popular piece of literature, still, everybody was convinced that it was an imaginative piece of work by Homer. Thus, when in the April of 1870, Schliemann and his new Greek bride, the 17-year old Sophia Engasteromenos –thirty years younger than himself – dug the first spade into the soil of Hisarlık, the whole world, including expert professors of archaeology, were laughing at them. Schliemann was not an archaeologist. However, he had two important traits: ambition and stubbornness, which he shared with similar adventurer scientists of his time, such as Howard Carter who discovered Tutankhamen, Robert Koldewey who rediscovered Babylon, and Austin Henry Layard, who found Nineveh. Also, he had something they probably did not have: plenty of money. Afterwards, Schliemann would say that his objective in the later period of his life was to discover Troia, Mycenae and Orchomenos, the three cities, which Homer refers to as *rich in gold* in the *Iliad*. He actually discovered Troia. Mycenae had been discovered, but it was again Schliemann who

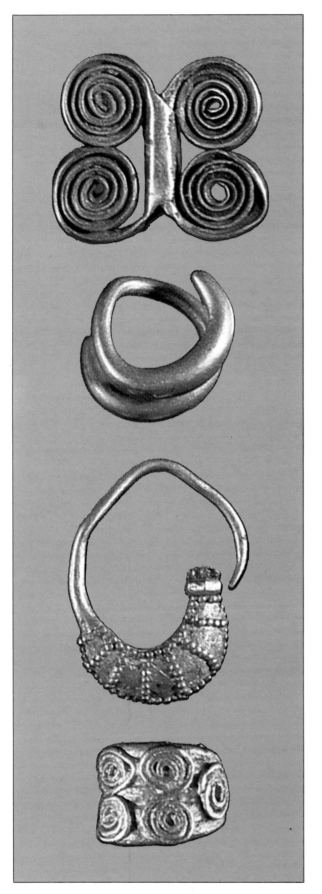

found the treasure attributed to the Mycenaean rulers. Orchomenos was his briefest and least successful enterprise.

The misfortune of Hisarlık is that it was the first excavation by Schliemann. He believed that the deeper he went, the greater his change of finding the giant towers, strong fortifications, temples, gold and silver, and bronze weapons Homers mentioned. By digging huge trenches which went through the site like a knife cutting large pieces out of a cake, he destroyed a very large portion of the tumulus. No archaeologist and no amount of effort or money can ever replace what has been lost at Troia. His contemporary colleagues, and other archaeologists who worked on the site after him, have never forgiven Schliemann for his haste and irresponsibility. Baked clay vessels, copper and bronze artefacts, and similar items had often been brought to light in various digs carried out in different parts of the world, but these alone would not have created the sensation and international recognition he was seeking. He was out to find a treasure, preferably the treasure of King Priam, or any treasure that he could attribute to King Priam's city. For this reason while he was digging, he was only interested in gold, and did not care that he was possibly throwing away the various layers of different settlements and anything relating to them*. In the end he found what he was looking for.

Schliemann, in his volume entitled *Troy, and Its Remains*, published in 1875, relates the events of the day he found the treasure with the following words.

In excavating this wall further... I came upon a large copper article of the most remarkable form, which attracted my attention all the more as I thought I saw gold behind it. On top of this copper article lay a stratum of red and calcinated ruins, as hard as stone, and above this again lay the above-mentioned wall of fortification... In order to withdraw the Treasure from the greed of my workmen, and to save it for archaeology, I had to be most expeditious, and although it was not yet time for breakfast, I immediately had paidos [restbreak] called... While the men were eating and resting, I cut out the Treasure with a large knife, which it was impossible

* Although the number of pieces which were lost is not known, when Schliemann kept records these were very carefully written and detailed.

Gold jewellery with spiral motifs and hair-rings. Troia II (2500–2200 BC). İstanbul Archaelogical Museums. Discovered by Schliemann, Dörtpfeld and Blegen

to do without the very great exertion and the most fearful risk of my life, for the great fortification wall, beneath which I had to dig, threatened every moment to fall down upon me. But the sight of so many objects, every one of which is of inestimable value of archaeology, made me foolhardy, and I never thought of any danger. It would, however, have been impossible for me to have removed the Treasure without the help of my dear wife, who stood by me ready to pack the things which I cut out in her shawl and to carry them away.

The first thing I found was a large copper shield...

The second object which I got out was a copper cauldron with two horizontal handles...

The third object was a copper plate...

Thereupon followed a globular bottle of the purest gold... Then came a cup, likewise of the purest gold.

Next came another cup of the purest gold...

When the objects in the treasury Schliemann discovered were summed up it emerges that it comprised copper and bronze cauldrons, cups and trays, bowls, spear heads, and similar artefacts of all kinds, and gold and electrum jewellery. The latter included gold rings, bracelets, earrings and two head pieces which were made of thousands of small pieces. Schliemann and his wife piled the riches, including the small chest key they had found at the same spot, into the shawl of Sophia and carried it home. They were still unable to believe in what they had found and were trembling with excitement. Once they were home they locked the door, pushed a chair against it and drew the curtains. They spread what they had found on the bed. They were very happy that the headpieces, which were made of tiny gold particles, had survived in a vase without being scattered into the soil. They kept snatching up each item and stroking it and trying it on. Once their excitement had abated somewhat, they pulled the big trunk in which Sophia kept some of her clothes out from under the bed. They wiped and cleaned each item of the treasury carefully, wrapped it in a piece of cloth, and placed it in the trunk.

There was nothing to prevent Schliemann from believing that the riches he had found did actually belong to King Priam. There was one disconcerting factor though, which did not quite match his theory; that was that the treasury had been found outside the city walls.

Gold ornamental pins. Troia II (2500–2200 BC). İstanbul Archaeological Museums. Discovered by Schliemann, Dörpfeld and Blegen

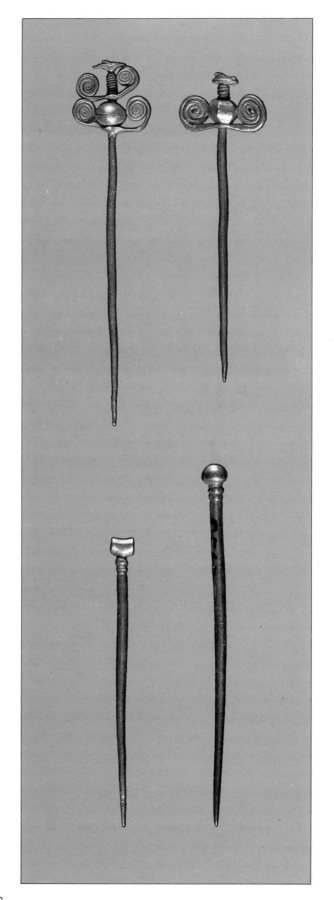

He has, however, found a key to a chest together with the gold, so he concluded that whoever had tried to carry the heavy chest outside the city when the fight was at its height must have thrown it down the foot of the city walls when he saw the Achaeans coming. Afterwards, it would have been covered in fire debris.

Time passed slowly after the discovery of the treasure. Both Schliemann and his wife thought that their workers had grown suspicious, when they were all of a sudden called off work on a Saturday, which should have been a normal working day. At last, the end of the excavation season came, and among the many trunks loaded with fragments of baked clay pottery and all sorts of marble and stone pieces, was the one containing the personal belongings of Schliemann's wife. This attracted no attention at all at the Ottoman customs. The same procedure was followed at the Piraeus customs and the trunk, which was never inspected during its journey, was driven to a safe house in Athens.

What happened to the treasure after that point is comparable to a James Bond film today. According to the agreement signed between Schliemann and the Ottoman Government, half of everything unearthed at the site had to be given to the government. From that time on, the Greek lawyers of Schliemann, and those of the Ottoman Government, were to meet frequently at the court of Athens. Although the Greek authorities had hoped that the treasure would stay in Greece forever, in a 'Schliemann Museum' that the archaeologist had suggested building, at the same time, they did not want to offend the Ottoman State. Meanwhile, Schliemann, fearing that Greek authorities would confiscate his treasure, moved it to the safe at the French Archaeological Institute in Athens. Before long, however, Schliemann accepted his liability to pay the Ottoman State a substantial sum of money – for that time – and return some of the pieces he had stolen, and so an agreement was reached. Schliemann also heard that the Ottoman authorities investigating the houses of the local people who had worked on the site, found gold pieces which had been removed from the excavations without the archaeologist's knowledge. He was furious!

Schliemann had proved his theory; his venture had been successful and he was now well-established and a man of fame. He received invitations from all four corners of the world; everyone competed for him to visit and give lectures. His diaries and excavation reports were published in different languages. The treasure was first put on display in London, while Schliemann negotiated the sale of it with the American authorities and the British Museum. Finally, to his Greek wife's disappointment, it ended up in the Ethnographical Museum which was then being built in Berlin.

When Schliemann eventually died, there were many people who thought his manner of dying was appropriate to the way he lived. He had been suffering in both ears for a long time. In addition to his medicines, he sometimes had to have an operation on them. One day in Naples, he left his hotel to investigate the latest digs at Pompeii. He collapsed in the street, and when he was found by the police he had no money or identification on him. By the time his identity was established and was given preferential treatment, it was too late, and he died.

The so-called 'Treasure of Priam' endured longer than its discoverer. Although it survived the World War I without incident, during the Second World War, when the Russian soldiers were approaching Berlin, it was hastily packed and hidden in a part of the zoo. When the war was over, very little of the zoo was left. The latest press news about the lost treasure is that some of its pieces were seen at the Pushkin Museum in Moscow. The gold pieces from the same treasure that are on display in İstanbul Archaeological Museums are those unearthed by Schliemann, Dörpfeld and by Professor Carl W. Blegen during the excavations he conducted for the University of Cincinatti between 1932 and 1938, together with some obtained through different channels.

THE TROJAN WAR

The story of the Trojan war has been dealt with in varying degrees – sometimes in whole from the beginning to the end, sometimes in part – by poets of antiquity such as Homer, Virgil, Aeschylus, and Sophocles. Boccacio, Chaucer, Shakespeare, Schiller, Racine, Giraudaux and T.S. Eliot are only a few of the writers who have dealt with the subject in later centuries.

When all the information from the separate texts of antiquity is brought together there is a consensus that the seed of the Trojan war was planted during a feast on Mount Olympus. The ancient bards would probably have begun reciting about the war with a few words about the legendary foundation of Troia, then continuing with the story of Helen of Sparta and the beauty contest on Mount Ida.

Ilios of Troas participates in the competitions organized by the King of Phrygia and wins the first prize. Among the gifts presented to him is a white cow with black spots. It walks along, at last stops at a place close to the sea, between the rivers Scamander and Simois. The city founded on this spot - in accordance with the oracle - is named Ilios after its founder, and later Troia, after Tros who was the ancestor of Ilios. After a time, Zeus drops a very large statue of Pallas Athena, 'Palladium', a spear in one hand and a distaff in the other, and Ilios founds the temple of Athena where it fell. The children and grandchildren of Ilios multiply abundantly, and lead happy and peaceful lives until the reign of King Priam.

When Helen of Sparta, who was conceived by Zeus – disguised as a swan – from Leda, reaches a

married to Menelaus, who succeeded Tyndareus as King of Sparta after his death.

The next step towards this tragic war is taken at the wedding of Peleus, the old king of Iolkus, and Tethys – the prettiest of the Nereids, the daughters of Nereus living at the bottom of the ocean. The goddess of envy and argument, Erys, being offended that she was not invited to the wedding, throws a golden apple with the words 'To the Most Beautiful' inscribed on it, onto the table at which sit Hera, Athena and Aphrodite. Zeus is not willing to take part in the quarrel that begins between his wife and two daughters. *Take Hermes with you* he says, *and ask him to guide you to Mount Ida. There is no mortal better equipped in matters of the heart, than the Trojan prince, Paris, who is tending his flocks there. If he cannot decide, nobody can. In addition to this, all the gods and goddesses are witness to the fact that he is an honest arbitrator.*

When Paris suddenly sees the three goddesses and Hermes in his cottage he is surprised and rightly,

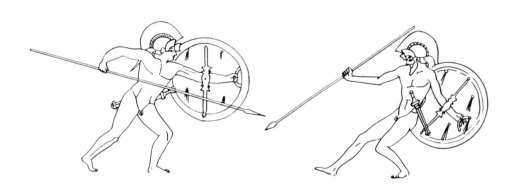

marriageable age, eligible suitors including Diomedes, Ajax, Patroclus, Odysseus and Menelaus, brother of King Agamemnon of Mycenae, all heroes of the Hellenic world, go to the palace of King Tyndareus. When the king realizes that any choice he might make will offend all the other suitors and even start a quarrel, the quick-witted Odysseus says *Let us step forward one by one, and swear an oath that whoever is chosen, the rest will pledge allegiance and protect his honour!* Although it is not known whether Helen herself, or her step-father chose out of the suitors seeking her hand in marriage, it is known that she was

scared. *Who am I to judge among such divine beauties?* he protests. Then, *Shall I cut the apple into three portions and share it among them? In this way, I probably wouldn't offend any of them.* However, Zeus has decided that one of them must be chosen, and no one can go against his decisions. In addition, the goddesses promise that whoever he chooses, the other two will not be angry and harm him.

This beauty contest, which took place in the shepherd's cottage of Paris on Mount Ida, was to be a subject of discussions for many years to come and was to be re-established towards the end of the twentieth

Marble head of Zeus. Third–second centuries BC. Troia IX. İstanbul Archaeological Museums

Aphrodite, the virgin goddess, who was born of the white foam of the waves at Paphos in Cyprus, approaches, puts her lips near the blushing young man and whispers, *There is no rush Paris. Nobody is chasing after you. Do not let your eyes miss anything'*, and, letting Paris take a deep breath, *But the moment I saw you, I said to myself, oh, the most handsome young man herding cattle on Mount Ida. Why, Paris? Why don't you move to the city and live a civilized life? What would you lose by marrying a woman like Helen of Sparta? If she let her eyes rest on you only once, I'm sure she would leave everything behind and follow you... What do you mean by saying that you have not heard of Helen of Sparta? Let me describe her beauty to you.*

In this way, Paris gives the golden apple to Aphrodite, and at that moment, the offended Hera and Athena decide to destroy Troia. After this, Aphrodite wastes no time in materializing the love scenario she

century AD. It was also to be the subject of many paintings, sculptures, mosaics and suchlike, and today of films. Some artists, such as Picasso for instance were to have the same instinct as Paris, and consider giving an apple to each goddess.

When Hermes, the three beauties and the arbitrator agree on the rules of the contest, it starts with Hera, the wife of Zeus. Letting her tunic fall to the ground, she says, *Listen to me, Paris*, and slowly walking in front of the young man to display her beauty, *examine all of me slowly, without rushing. You may command Asia, and become the richest man in the world.* Paris replies *I'm sorry, sacred divinity, I cannot accept bribes. I think I have seen all your beauty. Now, please put on your clothes. It is the turn of the divine Athena.*

Paris, begins Athena, *I know you are a very smart young man and know to whom you should give this apple.* While walking up and down in front of him naked, *It is for you to choose. Do you wish to become the most handsome man, the most intellectual person, and the most powerful warrior in the world?* Paris says *I am a humble shepherd, divine Athena, I know you have your share in the prevailing peace in Troas, and influence the welfare of the people in the kingdom of my father, Priam, but in this matter, please don't ask anything from me. Now, please pick up your robe, and if she is ready, let the divine Aphrodite step in.'*

had drawn for Paris and Helen. Paris is sent to Sparta as the Trojan envoy, and on his return to Troia he abducts Helen.

Bad news must have travelled fast even at that time for Menelaus hears the scandal in Crete, and cutting his business trip short, rushes home. Without wasting any time, he begins calling on the suitors who have sworn an oath of allegiance to him. Some time has passed since then however, and each of them is immersed in his own life. Some of them remember their oath and agree to join the army that Menelaus is trying to raise, but some, unwilling to die for Menelaus in a war far away from their homes, do not honour it.

Among the latter is Odysseus who has been forewarned by oracles that if he ever goes to Troia he will not return home for twenty years. When he hears that Menelaus calling him, he pretends that he has gone mad. He puts a weird hat on his head, harnesses an ox and a donkey to the plough, and starts spreading salt instead of seed on the land he tills. However, one of Menelaus' friends snatches Odysseus' son, Telemachus, from the arms of his mother, Penelope, who is silently watching the scene, and puts him in front of the plough. Odysseus has to stop in order not to kill his baby son, and he is unable to fool anyone anymore.

Tethys is another person who has learned from seers that her son would never come back from the Trojan expedition. When she hears that Menelaus is coming, she makes her son, Achilles, wear women's clothing and then hides him in the women's quarters of the palace. Odysseus adds a sword and a spear to the gifts he has piled in front of the women, and calls one of his friends to blow the war trumpets. Achilles, dressed as a woman, thinking that they are being attacked, springs out from among the womenfolk, and grabs the weapons that have been included with the gifts.

The Achaean fleet gathers at Aulis, and sets sail with the prevailing winds.

From the time trade first began, routes connecting the Aegean world, the Cyclades, the Mediterranean and mainland Greece to the Black Sea, had to go through the Hellespont, and merchant ships bearing cargoes of gold, amber, jade, cloth, hemp, yarn, dried fish, wine, olive oil, slaves, wood for shipbuilding and similar items, had to go through this passage controlled by Troia. The Trojans must have exacted taxes from these merchant ships, and it looks as if the Mycenaeans wanted to bring a permanent end to this Trojan monopoly of the northern trade route and, together with like minded rulers, started a Trojan campaign.

To make a long story short, the Achaean warships sacked the Aegean islands one by one, also the coast of Western Anatolia, and at long last reached the Hellespont. They beached their ships and set up camp. Among the epic poets who narrate the events of the campaign after this point, Homer should be the first.

The name of Homer has been heard in ancient literature from the seventh century BC. Herodot, the father of history, says that:

... for Homer and Hesiod are the poets who composed our theogonies and described the gods for us, giving them all their appropriate titles, offices,

Bard reciting an epic poem. The hall is modelled after Pylos palace, where King Nestor, one of the Achaean leaders who fought against Troia in the *Iliad*, lived. (illustration A. Tobey)

and powers, and they lived, as I believe, not more than four hundred years ago...

Since Herodot lived in about the middle of the fifth century BC, this means that Homer must have lived in the middle of the nineth century BC. Although more than one city has been claimed as his birthplace, that with the greatest claim is İzmir. The excavations carried out in Bayraklı, or Old Smyrna, have shown that the site in antiquity was a flourishing town, having close ties with the rest of the Aegean and the Mediterranean world. Homer was a link in the chain of oral poetry, a tradition which must have been established in the Aegean world a long time before he lived. During his time, that is the Dark Age, it is known that bards moved from the palace of one king to another, and recited wherever they were. According to the place, the times and the bard, the legends changed their shape, content or length. Homer is thought to have done the same, and thus created the *Iliad* and the *Odyssey*. It has also been suggested that a bard's life would not have been long enough to produce two such long books, and that they might therefore have been the joint venture of a group of bards following a Homeric school of tradition. While the *Odyssey* mainly narrates the wanderings of Odysseus, it makes frequent references to the Trojan war as well.

It is known that the *Iliad* was based on a already known poem named the *Wrath of Achilles*. It is made up of twenty four books and more than 16,000 verses, and it is thought that it would take a complete night to recite the poem. Its detail is often based on the actuality of the age in which the bard found himself (mid-nineth century BC), and does not agree with the times of the Trojan war (mid-thirteenth century BC). In addition to this, even though the bard is from Anatolia, at the time he lived his work would have been recited in the halls of the Greek rulers therefore, the Achaeans are treated like Trojan heroes. However, when the texts of the books are closely examined, the Anatolian character of the bard comes to the surface. To sum it up, while hypocrisy, lying and deceit underline the actions of most of the Achaean rulers, the Trojans are characterized by a sort of honesty and integrity. The massacre witnessed in Troia after the city fell which did not spare the children or women, was a characteristic feature of the Dark Age, rather than of the time when the Trojan war was fought.

It is assumed that after Homer's time, his works continued to be passed down from generation to generation, moved to mainland Greece, and were written down probably only in the seventh century BC. The *Iliad* starts with the rage of Achilles against Agememnon, and his withdrawal from the battlefield, and ends with the funeral of the Trojan hero, Hector. The topics of the each book can be summed up as follows:

Book I: Chryses, the priest of Apollo, comes to the Achaean camp to pay ransom for his daughter, Chryseis who is taken as a part of the war spoils. When his request is refused by Agamemnon, Apollo accepts his prayers and sends a plague to the Achaean camp. Agamemnon, in order to save his army, gives the priest's daughter back to him, but instead takes Briseis, another girl who has fallen to the share of Achilles. The latter becomes very angry and withdraws to his tent. On Mount Olympus, the gods discuss the war amongst themselves.

Book II: Zeus sends a false dream to Agamemnon, and makes him believe that he can capture Troia. The leader of the Achaean army brings together his commanders, and relates his dream to them. However, everyone is tired from the ten years taken by the war and longs to go home. Odysseus interferes, and changes the minds of his colleagues. They become heartened and move to the battlefield. The heroes in the Achaean lines and those in the Trojan ranks, are introduced one by one.

Book III: Paris, son of Priam, offers to fight Menelaus, whoever wins the fight taking Helen. Helen from a high point above the city, identifies the Achaean heroes she knows to King Priam. When Menelaos is about to kill Paris, Aphrodite interferes and surrounding him with a cloud spirits him away. She then takes Helen to Paris.

Book IV: Discussions between the gods on Olympus. At last Zeus grants permission to his wife to destroy Troia. War continues and plenty of Trojans die.

Book V: The lines of Trojans are scattered by Diomedes of Crete. With the assistance of Athena he wounds Aphrodite and Ares, who were both helping the Trojans, disguised as warriors.

Book VI: Hector returns to Troia from the battlefield and asks his mother, Hecuba, to go to the temple of Athena and dedicate gifts. Meanwhile, on the battlefield, Diomedes and Glaucus of Lycia – grandson of Bellerophon – challenge each other. When they discover that their families have long traditions of hospitality, they stop fighting and exchange their weapons as peace tokens, swearing everlasting friendship. Hector meets his wife, Andromache, in front of the city walls, and they talk.

Book VII: Hector moves to the battlefield and challenges the Achaeans. Big Ajax comes forward to accept the challenge. Neither can beat the other. Night descends, and both sides draw back and gather their dead; they clean and wash them. The Achaeans surround their camps with a wall, and dig a moat around it, with sharpened poles at the bottom.

Book VIII: Zeus decides to give the upperhand on the battlefield to the Trojans. The Achaean warriors are forced to withdraw to the moat. Hera scolds her husband for supporting the Trojans.

Book IX: Agamemnon gathers the Achaean leaders, and tells them he is now prepared to make peace with

Achilles. He is willing to give back the girl, Briseis, whom he has previously taken from him, plus other gifts as well. However, Achilles fury has not yet abated, the messengers return empty handed.

Book X: Odysseus and Diomedes from the Achaean side, and Dolon from the Trojan side, spy on each other's camp at night. Odysseus tricks Dolon, and learns from him the whereabouts of the camp of the Thracians — allies of Troia. Diomedes kills Dolon. The two heroes attack the Thracian camp, kill the soldiers, and steal their famous thoroughbred horses.

Book XI: On the battlefield Agamemnon and Diomedes do heroic deeds, however, in the end, the Trojans get the upper hand. The Achaeans decide if Patroclus wears the armour of Achilles and joins the war, the Trojans will take him for Achilles and draw back.

Book XII: Apollo diverts the waters of the rivers in the area including Scamander and Simois, to wards the wall around the Achaean camp. Hector breaks one of the walls with a piece of rock. The Trojans, some coming through the door, some jumping over the wall, attack the Achaeans.

Book XIII: The battle is taking place in front of the Achaean ships. Poseidon watches the battle *aloft the summit of timbered samos facing thrace* [Samothrace], and encourages the Achaenas.

Book XIV: The Trojans come very close to the Achaean ships. Agamemnon suggests that they should get on the ships and sail away. Hera sees that the situation is out of control, and things are going badly for the Achaeans. From Aphrodite, she borrows her famous breastband, which whets sexual appetite, and seduces Zeus. When Zeus falls asleep, Poseidon helps the Achaeans.

Book XV: Zeus wakes up and realizes that he has been deceived. He scolds Hera, moves Poseidon away from the battlefield, and sends Apollo to help Hector. The Trojans are about to burn the Achaean ships. Patroclus is unhappy about the way the battle is going.

Book XVI: Achilles' rage has still not yet abated. Despite this, he loans his armour to Patroclus. The latter attacks the Trojan lines and kills Sarpedon, the grandson of Bellerophon and leader of the Lycians. The Trojans begin to flee. Patroclus, who comes as close as the walls of Troia, is killed by Hector.

Book XVII: The war wages around the body of Patroclus. Hector strips the corpse and sends his weapons into Troia. Menelaus and Ajax manage to take the body of their compatriot to their camp. The horses of Achilles, which are harnessed to Patroclus' chariot, shed tears.

Book XVIII: Achilles is in deep sorrow. Tethys, his mother, goes to Hephaestus, and asks him for new weapons for her son. These arms are described in detail.

Book XIX: Hephaestus gives the arms to Tethys. Achilles and Agamemnon make peace. Briseis is given back with more gifts added. The approaching death of Hector and that of Achilles, which is to follow, is narrated.

Marble statue of river god Scamander. First-second centuries AD. Troia IX. İstanbul Archaeological Museums

Book XX: Zeus gathers all the gods and goddesses on Olympus, and tells them that each of them is free to help whichever side they choose. Apollo, Ares, Aphrodite and Leto are on the side of the Trojans. The Achaeans are supported by Hera, Athena, Hermes, Poseidon and Hephaestus. On the battlefield Aeneas comes forward to meet Achilles face to face and is saved by the interference of gods. The heroic deeds of Achilles on the battlefield are narrated.

Book XXI: Achilles kills the Trojans one by one, throwing their corpses into the river Scamander, and saying,

Nothing can save you now—
not even your silver-whirling, mighty-tiding river—
not for all the bulls you' ve slaughtered to it for years.

he mocks the rivers. They become furious and chase Achilles in front of their waves.
(This is an interesting part of the *Iliad*, and it gives the impression that Homer, the bard, by using the uprising of the streams, has made clear his own protest at these foreign nations, which had been continuously pillaging and plundering the coasts of Anatolia.)

taking a man's shape, its voice breaking out of a whirlpool:
'Stop, Achilles! Greater than any man on earth,
greater in outrage too—
for the gods themselves are always at your side!
But if Zeus allows you to kill of all the Trojans,
drive them out of my depths at least, I ask you,
out on the plain and do your butchery there.
All my lovely rapids are crammed with corpes now,
no channel in sight to sweep my currents out to sacred sea—
I'm choked with corpses and still you slaughter more,

you blot out more! Leave me alone, have done—'
...
...and the river charged agaist him,
churning, surging, all his rapids rising in white fury
and drove the mass of corpses choking tight his channel, the ruck Achilles killed—Scamander heaved them up and bellowing like a bull the river flung them out on the dry land but saved the living, hiding them down the fresh clear pools of his thundering whirling current but thrashing over Achilles' shoulders raised a killerwave—

Achilles saves himself through the fire which Hephaestus starts to scare the streams. They return to their normal riverbeds. On Olympus there is quarreling and fighting among the gods. The Trojans retreat to their city.

Book XXII: Hector is the only one left outside the city walls. He takes no heed of the warnings of Priam and Hecuba, and after some heartsearching he decides to face Achilles. The latter kills Hector and drags his corpse behind his chariot, seven times around the walls of Troia. The Trojans are in deep mourning. Andromache shed tears for her dead husband.

Book XXIII: The Achaeans cease fighting, and prepare the burial ceremony of Patroclus. Wood is brought from the mountains to prepare the pyre for the dead hero. Competitions are organized, and winners receive valuable prizes.

Book XXIV: Priam, carrying gifts, goes to the

Ransom of the body of Hector. Red-figure skyphos by Brygos painter. *c* 480–470 BC. Kunsthistroisches Museen, Vienna. King Priam is accompanied by his servants bearing the ransom. Achilles is shown on a kline with Hector's body under it.

tent of Achilles to bring back the dead body of his son. Achilles gives him Hector's body, and stops the war until he has been buried. The *Iliad* finishes with the pyre and funeral of Hector:

and for nine days hauled in a boundless store of timber.

...

and they placed his corpse aloft the pyre's crest, flung a torch and set it all aflame.
Then they collected the white bones of Hector —
They placed the bones they found in a golden chest, shrounding them round and round in soft purple cloths. They quickly lowered the chest in a deep, hollow grave and over it piled a cope of huge stones closely set, then hastily heaped a barrow, posted lookouts all around for fear the Achaean combat troops would launch their attack before the time agreed. And once they'd heaped the mound they turned back home to Troy, and gathering once again they shared a splendid funeral feast Hector's honor, held in the house of Priam, king by will of Zeus.

And so the Trojans buried Hector breaker of horses.

The *Iliad* deals only with a limited part of the Trojan war. Nevertheless, the war continues. The Amazon queen Penthesilea, accompanied by a group of her female warriors, the Amazons comes to the aid of Troia. She performs heroic deeds, but is killed by Achilles. Among those who come to aid Troia is Memnon, the king of Ethiopia. He is to kill the Achaean hero Antilochus, but he himself will be killed by Achilles. Then it is turn of Achilles. Paris deals him a fatal blow with a bowshot, striking him in his only vulnerable spot, the heel of his right foot.

Now eulogies are sung in the Achaean camp for Achilles and competitions are organized. His body is burned with great ceremony. The remains are mingled with those of Patroclus, his best companion, and buried at Cape Siegum. Afterwards, a memorial in the shape of a tumulus is erected from soil.

After the death of Achilles, dividing his weapons poses a problem. When Agamemnon decides to share them between Menelaus and Odysseus, Ajax becomes furious, and plans to attack his comrades at night. Athena sends madness to Ajax. With a sword in hand, the maddened hero attacks the livestock gathered at the camp and slaughters them. In the end falling on his sword, he commits suicide.

At this part of the war Paris is killed by Philoktetes,

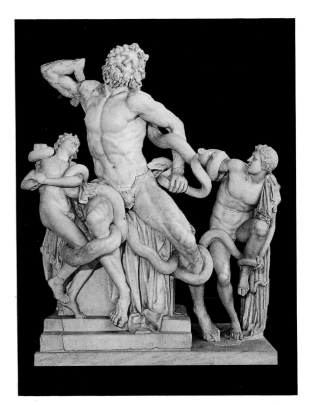

Marble statue of Laocoon and his sons by Hagesandros, Polydoros and Athanodoros. *c* 175–150 BC. Vatican Museum. The seer of Troia, Laocoon warns his friends not to trust the Achaeans and destroy the wooden horse. However, two serpents sent by Apollo emerge from the sea and crush him and his sons to death for in the past the seer had insulted the god by making love to his wife in front of the god's statue. The event makes the Trojans to think that Laocoon was punished by god for having insulted the wooden horse, a gift dedicated to Athena and consequently they decide to carry it into their city.

but the Trojans still refuse to give Helen up. The Achaeans learn that as long as Palladium, the statue of Pallas Athena, which has been in the temple since its foundation, stands there, Troia is not to fall. Odysseus, pretending that he is a slave running from the Achaeans, shelters in the city and steals the statue.

The war continues with the story of the wooden horse. In the end, the Achaean soldiers slaughter all the citizens of Troia not even sparing the women and children. The only person to escape the massacre is Aeneas and his aged father. His wanderings were to be narrated in detail in the great work of Virgil (70–19 BC), the Aeneid. At the end of the book, Aeneas reaches Latium, today's Italy and by founding Lavinium there, plants the seeds of the Roman Empire.

VISITORS TO TROIA

Troia along with the Pyramids, has been the most popular sightseeng spot since antiquity. Throughout the ages it is well known that visitors to the Troas region have never missed the opportunity of going to Troia, whether they be kings, queens, famous commanders, or just humble citizens.

Among these the earliest known is Xerxes (485–465 BC), the Persian ruler. According to Herodotus, on his way to conquer Europe in the 480s BC, the king stopped here,

During a night in camp at the foot of Mt Ida a heavy storm of thunder and lightning caused the death of a considerable number of men. When the army reached the Scamander, the first river since the march from Sardis began which failed to provide enough water for men and beasts, Xerxes had a strong desire to see Troy, the ancient city of Priam. Accordingly he went up into the citadel, and when he had seen what he wanted to see and heard the story of the place from the people there, he sacrificed a thousand oxen to the Trojan Athena, and the Magi made libations of wine to the spiritis of the great men of old.

In common with everybody else Alexander the Great also visited Troia in 333 BC – during his eastern expedition. He believed himself to be descended from Achilles, and he is said to have kept a copy of the *Iliad* under his pillow. While crossing from Sestos to Abydos (from Eceabat to Çanakkale) at the prow of his flagship, he sacrificed a bull to the sea god, Poseidon, when halfway across, and before his ship had been properly beached, he shot his lance and thrust it into the soil of Asia, claiming it for himself. Afterwards he went to Achilles' tumulus, annointed himself and ran three times naked around the grave* – an act which was imitated about five hundred years later by the Roman Emperor Caracalla. When the Trojans of the time gave Alexander the Great the lyre which once belonged to Paris, he is said to have remarked, *I don't care I came here for the lyre on which Homer says Achilles used to sing of his heroic deeds and achievements.* Then he added that he regarded the hero as very lucky for having such a bard as Homer, who immortalized his achievements. When he saw that the offspring of the river Scamander, which once chased Achilles in front of its waves, was no more than a rivulet that he could easily jump across and Ajax' shield which was *seven-fold, brass bound* according to Homer was no more than a round piece of armour, he was too polite and taken back to make deragotary remarks. Going to the temple of Athena, he dedicated his own arms and he took those claimed to have been used by the heroes who died in the Trojan war. Although it is not known whether or not these arms, were original, he took them with him even to the most distant corners of India. He is known to have made generous gifts to the temple, and his interest in Troia passed, after his death, to his general Lysimachus.

In later centuries, Julius Caesar wanted to see the place whence his Trojan ancestor, Aeneas, came, and in 48 BC he visited the site. It is said that when he saw that the original home of his ancestors was just a poor, neglected hill covered with bushed and goat droppings, he was very disappointed and lost interest. Nevertheless,

---

* In the *Iliad*, the burial of Patroclus gives some idea about the grave mounds erected above graves themselves. At the end of the poem, the Trojans erect a similar memorial for Hector. Often the soldiers who died on the foreign soil were cremated there. It is said that the tombs of Achilles, Ajax, Antiochos and Patroclus were intended to become well-known landmarks in the Troas. Today, the mounds which are attributed to the fallen heroes of the Trojan war are thought in fact to have been erected much later than that period and must have belonged other people. Research has shown that these particular mounds contained no graves of any sort. Also, the *Iliad* puts the remains of Achilles and Patroclus into the same grave, not into separate ones. Wind and rain or other forces of nature have worn these mounds down, so they are nothing like their original impressive height.

he is known to have granted it independence and exemtion from taxes.

It has already been mentioned that before deciding finally on Byzantium as his new capital, the Roman Emperor, Constantine the Great, had considered establishing it hereabouts at Cape Sigeum. Emperor Julian the Apostate (AD 361–63) relates in his memoirs that when he visited Troia during still kept burning in memory of the heroes of the Trojan war.

One of the latest historic figures to visit Troia, was Sultan Mehmet II, the Conqueror (1451–81). His visit to Troia is recorded by his contemporary, the Greek historian, Critoboulos of Imbros. He says that walked around the fortifications of the site,

...inspected its ruins, saw its topographical advantages, and its favourable position close to the sea and the opposite continent. Then he asked to be shown the tombs of the heroes Achilles, Hector and Ajax, and like other great conquerors before him he made offerings at the tomb of Achilles, congratulated him on his fame and his great deeds, and on having found the poet Homer (whom Cyriac had read to Mehmet) to celebrate them. Then, it is said, he pronounced these words: 'It is to me that Allah has given to avenge this city and its people: I have overcome their enemies, ravaged their cities... Indeed it was the Greeks who before devastated this city, and it is their descendants who after so many years have paid me the debt which their boundless pride [hubris] had contracted – and often afterwards – towards us, the peoples of Asia.

The other visitors to Troia are too many to include here. Among the popular nineteenth century visitors Lady Mary Wortley Montague, Charles T. Newton, Lord Byron and J.C. Hobhouse can be mentioned.

ÇANAKKALE ARCHAEOLOGICAL MUSEUM

The present Museum of Çanakkale was opened in 1984, and its collections, although not very large, including interesting articles found in the excavations carried out in Troas region. Ob jects coming from the various settlement layers of Troia are displayed chronologically, and there are also interesting items on display from such ancient sites as Dardanos, Assos, and the island of Tenedos.

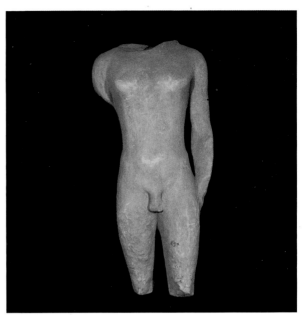

Marble statue of kouros. End of fifth century BC. Lampsacos. Çanakkale Archaeological Museum

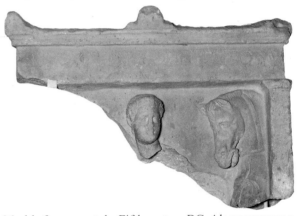

Marble funerary stele. Fifth century BC. Alecopennessos, Gallipoli. Çanakkale Archaeological Museum

Baked clay oil flasks (lekytoi). Sixth-ninth centuries BC. Çanakkale Archaeological Museum

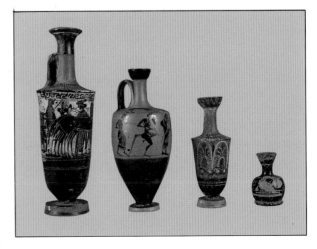